WHAT
MEN
WISH
YOU
KNEW

THE 40 RULES
TO ATTRACT A MAN
AND KEEP HIM

JARRED JAMESON

CONTENTS

INTRODUCTION 1

PART ONE 6

The Secrets To Attracting A Man 6
    RULE ONE 8
    RULE TWO 12
    RULE THREE 16
    RULE FOUR 20
    RULE FIVE 24

PART TWO 28

The First Few Dates 28
    RULE SIX 30
    RULE SEVEN 34
    RULE EIGHT 37
    RULE NINE 40
    RULE TEN 43
    RULE ELEVEN 47
    RULE TWELVE 51
    RULE THIRTEEN 55

PART THREE 58

The Thrill Of The Chase 58
    RULE FOURTEEN 61
    RULE FIFTEEN 65
    RULE SIXTEEN 69

PART FOUR 72

Understanding Male Behavior 72

RULE SEVENTEEN 75

RULE EIGHTEEN 79

RULE NINETEEN 83

RULE TWENTY 87

RULE TWENTY ONE 90

RULE TWENTY TWO 93

RULE TWENTY THREE 96

RULE TWENTY FOUR 98

RULE TWENTY FIVE 101

RULE TWENTY SIX 104

PART FIVE 107

Secrets Of The Bedroom 107

RULE TWENTY SEVEN 110

RULE TWENTY EIGHT 113

RULE TWENTY NINE 116

PART SIX 119

Dos & Don'ts 119

RULE THIRTY 121

RULE THIRTY ONE 124

RULE THIRTY TWO 127

RULE THIRTY THREE 130

RULE THIRTY FOUR 132

RULE THIRTY FIVE 136

RULE THIRTY SIX 139

RULE THIRTY SEVEN 142

RULE THIRTY EIGHT 145

RULE THIRTY NINE 148

RULE FORTY 151

CONCLUSION 154

INTRODUCTION

So, you want to attract a good man and keep him. But, so far, you have struggled with the task. Maybe you have even read a few other books on dating and they gave you advice like this:

"Make sure you smile. Men like women who smile."

"Make yourself available for him to approach you."

"Wear nice clothes so he will notice you."

"Update your dating profile with some good photos."

Blah blah blah blah blah.

Guess what? All that is superficial nonsense and will not get you the relationship you truly deserve.

The fact is, even if you have very few superficial qualities, you can still find a man. It doesn't matter if you are tall, short, fat or skinny. It doesn't matter what color your skin is. It doesn't matter whether you have a nice voice or an annoying one. It doesn't matter whether you are rich or flat broke. You can find a man. But the problem is, will it be the honorable, virtuous and committed guy that you are looking for and deserve?

I hear you saying: "But how? What am I doing wrong?"

Well, that's exactly what this book is about. This is a no-bullsh*t guide to getting a man and keeping him. This book is packed with 40 uncommon insights from a male perspective that, if you follow them, will help you secure a man — what's more, it will be the kind of man that you want to keep for the long term. This is a rare look inside the head of men.

Now, I want to be upfront with you. This book isn't always going to be polite. It isn't going to spare your feelings. If you are a fragile, little flower, then you might want to buck up a little before you read this. This book isn't here to coddle you. This book is here to speak truth to the woman who is truly fed up with all of the frankly rotten advice they keep getting. It is a guide to finding out what men really think about them, and how they can use this knowledge to their advantage.

If you can handle the brutal truth, tweak a few things and adjust your approach, then you will have your choice of men out there.

Why You Have Failed So Far

So, if it's so simple, why have you failed in your efforts to attract the perfect guy so far?

The answer is simple: you have been getting misleading advice. Most of what you have been reading and following in magazines and on websites is tame, recycled and politically correct garbage. You could make your own list of things to change about yourself to attract the perfect guy and get closer to the truth about relationships than you would following the advice you read on the internet. What you are reading is probably what a freelance writer found on some internet dating advice website and rehashed for a few bucks. In other words, it is not effective at all in the real world.

There is so much fluff out there that it can be difficult to navigate to the truth. But this book is completely different to anything else you have read on the subject matter. Unlike that lowly paid writer who only wants a quick turnaround for his recycled article, I'm not concerned about touching on controversial topics or sparing your feelings when it comes to delivering the truth. I couldn't care less if you get offended by the advice in this book.

In fact, I hope you do. At least you will finally open your eyes to the true lay of the land.

The advice in this book is for the woman who is so fed up with not being able to secure or keep a good man that she is willing to be offended to finally get some advice that makes sense. This book is intended to speak truth to the woman who is ready to hear it. If that's not you, well, too bad. Give it to someone who is ready for the truth!

No Bullsh*t Means Leaving Your Preconceptions At The Door

I'll make a deal with you. I promise not to spew any of that garbage dating advice that has been getting you nowhere and give you just the straight-up facts that will help you land the guy of your dreams and hold onto him for the long term. But in return, you have to leave all of your fixed notions and mental baggage at the door and be open to a new way of thinking. Don't bring your excuses, your hang-ups or anything else that is going to keep you from achieving your relationship goals.

Let's just agree that we are entering no-bullsh*t zone from now on.

Okay, ready? Then let's get started.

PART ONE

The Secrets To Attracting A Man

So, you want to attract the man of your dreams? This section is about exactly that. There are certain things that women do that actually alienate them from decent guys because they are so used to thinking of themselves in a certain way. You need to get past that and allow yourself to consider a new self-image — one that raises your value.

Attracting a guy is not difficult. Guys are visual creatures. Any man who sees a woman he finds attractive is probably going to want to talk to her. If she gives some sort of signal or sign that she is interested, then he is even more willing to talk to her — because the chance of rejection has gone down.

But what kind of guys are you actually attracting?

Many women find that they have no problem

getting guys to talk to them, but once they start talking, they discover the guys are not worth their time or have very little to offer in terms of a long-term relationship. These guys do nothing for your life. They don't help you achieve your goals and they don't support you when you need support the most. These are unreliable men that you should avoid at all costs. They are a time sink and are only interested in you physically.

You probably already know this to a certain extent. It is impossible for a woman to go through life and not realize that guys are visual. You've seen them do a double take when a certain type of woman walks into the room. But what you might not realize is that there is a lot more to catching the *right* man's eye than just having the correct body type or curves in the right places.

This section of the book is all about teaching you how to be more attractive to the man of your dreams — the person you want in your life. This is the first step in any interaction. Before you can charm him with the rest of the advice in this book, you have to attract his attention. Luckily, men, as we know, are very visual and this is fairly easy to do. You just need to perfect your technique, and that's exactly what this first section is about.

RULE ONE

Don't Be like Everyone Else

Everybody seems obsessed these days with being just like everybody else. Everyone wants to be seen wearing the clothes that are meant to be on trend, watching the same television shows and listening to the same music that their friends are into. Even to the point of driving the same cars and consuming the same food at the same restaurants, all in an effort to conform.

Well, guess what? Conformity isn't all that attractive.

When you're trying to follow somebody else, what you are basically doing is trying to co-opt that person's personality. You are trying to turn yourself into a clone of that person in an effort to achieve the same popularity and social status. We do this unconsciously and in thousands of different ways every day. We do this through the things that we say and repeat on social media, the way that we interact verbally and nonverbally with friends and strangers, the way that we change our behavior depending on the group of people we are with, and in lots of other ways.

But what women need to understand is that for

guys, sometimes the really unusual flavor that stands out from the crowd is the one that is going to be the most attractive. If you walk into an ice cream shop and all that's available is a huge row of slightly different variations of vanilla, after a few days of visiting that same ice cream shop you will definitely perk up if you hear about the rocky road flavor down the road — or the sherbet, or even plain old chocolate.

So, how and why do you avoid conforming with others?

It all comes down to one of the main themes of this book. It comes down to confidence.

Once you have the confidence of knowing who you are, then you don't have to be like anybody else. You could be unusual and different because that's who you are. You know that while everyone else is dyeing their hair blonde, you prefer to keep yours dark. You know that while all your friends are buying expensive cars, you prefer to spend your money on a good bike and save the environment. You don't care that your friends might judge you for this. You know who you are, and that, to a guy, can be incredibly sexy.

In a high school environment, this groupthink is

much more pronounced and difficult to overcome. That's because everyone in high school, to some degree or another, is at a vulnerable stage. Everyone is going through some phase of development, and things are happening to their body and mind that they don't really understand. But once you get out of high school and into a college environment, or start living your life as an adult, then it becomes less important to be part of a group. In fact, you want to stand out from the rest because you want to be chosen for the right job or get the promotion that everyone else is going for.

Men can recognize when a woman is trying to be like someone else — or trying to conform to a mainstream ideology — and it isn't very attractive. In fact, most guys will sweep right over the woman who is trying to be a clone of her friends. After all, how do you choose between a group of clones? If they all talk the same, wear the same accessories and seem to have the same personality, then most guys will be off looking for something more interesting. Nonconformity is far more interesting. When you encounter someone who doesn't care what other people think and who prefers to do things their way instead of how other people consider the right way, then you've come across a woman you can respect and appreciate for her uniqueness.

The more mature and open-minded a guy is, the more he is going to respect uniqueness and nonconformity in the women that he dates. Some guys go into the dating market thinking that they are looking for a tall blonde with bubbly personality traits and then find that the woman they actually fall in love with is so completely unexpected that they would never have been able to predict what she looked like beforehand. They were taken by the uniqueness.

So the bottom line here is to not be afraid to be yourself. You are your own person, with your own unique personality, and you want to find a guy who will appreciate your individual qualities and give you the love and respect that you deserve.

RULE TWO

Have Defined Goals

If you meet a woman and ask her what her plans for the future are, or what her goals might be, and she doesn't appear to have a plan or any solidified goals, then most good guys are going to move on and find someone more interesting.

No one out there wants to date a person who is a loser. No one wants to date someone without a purpose in life. There are women who devote their entire lives to pleasing a man. While that seems like the greatest thing ever on the surface, the truth is that it sucks. No respectable guy wants a woman who has no other interests in life other than him. No guy wants to be obsessed over. The only guys that you are going to get attention from when you open yourself up like this are abusers and manipulators. These are the types of guys who look for women they can control, because they get off on that control.

You obviously are not looking for an abuser when you go out seeking to date. You are looking for someone who wants to be with you for you. But ask yourself what your goals in life are . Do you want to become a famous painter? Do you want a career in addition to a family? Maybe you just want to start a work-at-home side hustle. It doesn't matter what your goals are, as long as you are passionate about something.

There is something really exciting about a woman who has goals and dreams — and the drive to achieve them. As men, we can be her partner in this endeavor, but there is no way that she will let us stand in her way. There is something incredibly sexy about that.

On the other hand, there is nothing more disappointing than a woman who doesn't seem to have any life goals whatsoever. She may already be wealthy and have an expense account, but if she only lives for shopping and partying then most decent guys are going to get bored very quickly or skip her altogether.

Real men, men who have matured past the point of wanting to party all the time, are going to be looking for a like-minded mate. They want someone who is in the same place as them in life. Someone who has dreams that they want to bring into reality. Someone who has hopes for the future. Someone that they can support in their struggles and who will support them in theirs. While there may still be a certain amount of partying going on between you, there will also be a great deal of passionate discussion about your interests and where you both are heading in life. This makes for a very strong bond.

Women who have a passion, especially creative women, are particularly fascinating. It can be very easy to become bored by someone who doesn't have any passions except for perhaps a few television shows. But someone who is well-rounded and has lots of different interests in many areas is going to be an interesting person to go out on dates with, visit foreign countries with and just to spend time with in general.

Another thing you may not realize is that if there is nothing that a guy can talk to you about that makes you completely explode with passion, he is not going to look at you as a very passionate lover. Someone that doesn't even have passion for the things that they like most in life is not going to have a great deal of passion for lovemaking and the way that they treat their partner either.

If you do not currently have any goals, then you should sit down for some serious thinking time and decide what it is that you love to do. How are you planning on paying for housing, food, utilities, transportation and other expenses? Is it by pursuing a dream career? Do you want to leave a mark on the world in some area of endeavor? Is there some sort of creative expression that you have fallen in love with? This may include anything from creating props for a movie set to being the chief executive officer of a Fortune 500 company. Passion is still passion, in whatever field.

Whatever your passion, if he is a genuine and virtuous guy then he will respond favorably to your enthusiasm and support you in it. The wrong kind of guy will not give two hoots what goals you have because he's not looking at the long term and he's not interested in building anything with you. So now you also have a great way to weed out the losers from your dating pool! Expressing passion is a win-win.

RULE THREE

Dress Sharply Rather Than Provocatively

OK, trigger warning with this one.

As guys, we're not sure what the deal is with some women's insistence on dressing provocatively. There is a big difference between dressing up nice for a night on the town and dressing provocatively so that you attract the attention of men with exposed cleavage, little to no leg coverage, bare midriffs, etc.

The truth is, if you are looking to get laid, dressing like this will probably get you that result. Will you like and respect the person that you go home with the next day? Probably not. The bottom line is that if you dress like that and someone takes you home, then the next day he is still going to consider you in the context of how he first met you, even if you dress in perfectly normal clothing afterwards. Even more disturbing, you are going to go on the backburner of guys who do this all the time for their next booty call. They are not going to show up at your door with flowers and a limo to take you out to a nice dinner or a picnic in the park.

They're going to show up at 3AM, completely wasted, begging you for your special brand of loving.

So, why do women continue dressing in ways that they know attract the wrong sorts of guys? One reason has to do with confidence. If you notice, a lot of what we are discussing here has to do with confidence. Often, women dress revealingly because they believe that they will not be able to attract a guy if they are dressed like they were going to a Tuesday afternoon book club. They put on way too much makeup because they falsely believe that their face is unattractive without it.

Well, here's the cold truth for you. Women who dress sparingly are not going to be treated well. They are not going to get much respect from the guys they attract, and they are not going to be able to attract guys that *they* respect. Women who dress sharp but with restraint, on the other hand, are going to be overlooked by those guys out there looking for an easy score. But they will get noticed by the types of guys they really want to meet. These are the types of guys who will take you out to a picnic in the park, who are not afraid of commitment, who are not using you for 3AM booty calls and who are generally decent, kind and respectful. They are the kind of guys that you would call "boyfriend material".

But does dressing sharp mean that you cannot look sexy when you go out? Should you avoid trying to accentuate your best features? Of course not. But you have to do it the right way, and it's a fine line. Just a hint of subtle sexiness can go a long way if you are dressed sharply. If you are wearing something that subtly shows off your curves without being too obvious, then guys are still going to take notice but they are going to respect you a lot more. The wrong kinds of guys will be unwilling to approach you because you'll appear to have a great deal of respect for yourself and are unlikely to swallow their spiel or be manipulated.

The fact is, good guys do not want to see all of your nooks and crannies right away. If there is no mystery left, then a few minutes of staring is going to give him the full picture. But the woman who is sharply dressed, has confidence and is hinting sexiness is going to drive men crazy because there is a mystery there that they want to solve. That's just how we are as human beings. Guys will spend time browsing the web because they heard a rumor that their favorite actress, who never wears revealing clothing or does any nude or partially nude scenes, has made a movie with a topless scene. Guys will literally spend hours going through various websites, Instagram posts and more just to solve the mystery. That's exactly what you need to do when you go out. You need to dress sharp, show them that you respect yourself and give them a mystery to solve.

RULE FOUR

Gain Feminine Confidence

We have already gone over confidence in the introduction of this book as well as in most parts so far. However, as it is the most important concept in this book, it is worth going over again. In this chapter we're going to focus on "feminine confidence". This section is all about attracting the guy that *you* want. No woman out there wants to date a loser. No one wants someone who is violent, abusive, withdrawn or suffers from major issues that simply do not contribute to a healthy relationship. But in order to avoid guys with these issues, you have to show that you have supreme confidence in yourself.

Confidence is like a force field the scares away insecure guys, including those who are verbally or physically abusive and men who are immature or extremely insecure in themselves. For people such as this, the only way they can mask their own insecurities is by finding someone who has less self-confidence than they do. If you have self-confidence, and you exude that self-confidence, these types of guys are going to avoid you like the plague. You're going to have a built-in shield that will simply repel them from your life. Even if you have had past relationships with these types of guys, just gaining a little bit of confidence will put you on a completely different level.

However, there is a difference between general confidence and feminine confidence. Actually, you might put it another way. You might say that there is a difference between masculine confidence and feminine confidence. For example, even though our culture strives for equality, men still ask women out more often than the other way around. Men still pay for dates more often, men initiate the first kiss and other physical contact, and lots of other little things that you may not think about.

But feminine confidence is something a little different. Feminine confidence means knowing that you are sexy and attractive. Feminine confidence means being able to look guys in the eye when they look at you because you know that you have nothing to fear. Creating feminine confidence tells everyone around you that you deserve an amazing relationship with the best possible guy out there, and that you have extremely high standards and you will never settle for a loser.

The question is, how do you develop that

confidence? It certainly isn't easy, but it can be developed over time by first recognizing that you have just as much value as anyone else who walks the earth. It also comes from recognizing that you are good at what you do, whether that be at work or for a hobby, and that you deserve the happiness that you strive for. It comes from knowing yourself and liking yourself. It also means that you cannot look to other people to validate your self-worth.

Little things can improve your feminine confidence. Wearing nice clothes that show you respect yourself is one of the ways in which it can improve; having goals and actually achieving them, and making exercise and a healthy diet part of your life can also contribute. There are many other ways which I describe later in this book that will allow you to build that feminine confidence.

Once you have a little bit of confidence, you will begin to choose better relationships, and each one of those will build your confidence even further. The same holds true for the opposite scenario. The more you enter into relationships without confidence and it inevitably turns out bad, the less confident you will become — which will result in more terrible relationships.

The fact is, feminine confidence is simply the natural progression from insecure feelings that everyone feels as a teenager or young adult to the confidence that begins to grow as you stack up accomplishments in your life and begin to forge your identity. This form of confidence is a magnet to equally confident and mature men, and acts as a barrier to those who wish to use you for their own ends.

Before you enter the dating arena it is important that you build up this confidence in yourself. It will act as your shield and protect you from negative people and relationships.

RULE FIVE

Smart Is Really Sexy

Contrary to what you might have heard, smart and confident women are sexy. If a guy thinks that intelligence is not a sexy attribute, then it is likely that he is suffering from some form of self-esteem issues himself and he feels threatened by a woman's intelligence.

Smart, intelligent and decent guys are not going to be threatened by a woman with brains. In fact, they are going to seek out women with intelligence. Meanwhile, dumb, insecure guys are going to seek out women who are — or at least they think are — unintelligent or unsophisticated. This allows those guys to control these women.

So, how do you know if you are smart or dumb? Actually, if you have to ask this question, then the odds are that you are pretty smart. Unintelligent people do not ask the question. They do not worry about this sort of thing. There are very few unintelligent women out there anyway, and it would be at about the same ratio as unintelligent men. However, there is a huge proportion of intelligent women that allow themselves to be manipulated and controlled by men.

Part of this has to do with looks. It can be easy to melt in the presence of someone with a great body and a cute face. Believe me, I know. We guys do the same thing. We often worship the idol of the beautiful blonde with the perfect body until we realize that there is nothing there except for that superficial attraction. Hopefully, you are able to discover very quickly that even if you can attract an incredible-looking man, you may not be satisfied if he is a moron.

The bottom line here is that you do not have to hide your intelligence. Many women think that they have to conceal certain things about themselves. They might hide the fact that they read a lot of books. They might hide the fact that they go to comic book conventions and have extensive knowledge of certain fandoms, such as learning languages from *Lord of the Rings,* or being able to quote from every single episode of *Star Trek: The Next Generation.* This is nothing to be ashamed of. To the right kind of guy, it is actually a wonderful and unique attribute.

Dumb guys are ashamed of themselves when they hang around smart women because clever women usually make more money than they do, have clearer ideas about the world, understand things better and are more mature than they are. Dumb guys feel the need to put down smart women because they often feel that women are inferior to men no matter what. When they run across a woman who clouds this narrow worldview, they are often unable to cope and respond by lashing out. Unfortunately, many smart women fall into this trap and end up dumbing themselves down so that they can attract a partner.

Please do not do this. For one thing, what you're doing is basically cutting off a part of yourself for someone else. Imagine that most of the guys out there had four fingers on each hand but you had five. Those five fingers give you better grip, more physical strength, the ability to complete tasks faster and a number of other advantages. But when a guy comes along with only four fingers, they immediately begin to belittle you because of your two extra fingers. Would you cut off those fingers, either figuratively or literally, to please a guy? That's what you are doing when you dumb yourself down for someone.

There are a lot of guys out there who are really smart and are striving to meet an equally smart woman. There are even guys out there who are not as smart as the women they date, but are mature enough and have enough respect for the woman that they can defer to them for their intelligence without feeling insecure.

But you really want to be alert for guys who believe they are superior to you just because they are male, and cannot accept that a woman might be smarter than they are. Those are the kinds of guys who are going to bring you down and make you downplay your intelligence, which is going to lead to an unhappy life.

Smart is really sexy. But not only that, for the intelligent guy, smart is a prerequisite in any potential partner. You want to make sure that you do not see your intelligence as some sort of curse. It is absolutely a blessing, and any guy who does not appreciate you for it should be off your radar immediately.

PART TWO

The First Few Dates

In this section we will be discussing some of the things you need to know for the first few dates that you go on with the guy you are interested in. The first few dates are critical. During them, each of you will be judging the other and noticing every detail. As a woman, you will probably notice more than the guy: but do not let that fool you into thinking that he doesn't notice anything or isn't perceptive. He is going to notice when you laugh at his jokes, when you do not understand something that he has said but try to fake it, or when you respond or pull away from him either verbally or physically.

Of course, this is also your chance to evaluate him and decide if this is a relationship you want to pursue. Many times, someone we have a crush on turns out to have a completely different personality than we expect and they become less attractive to us. You want to make sure that you allow for this possibility.

These chapters contain tips to keep in mind as

you are going out on dates. They include tips on how to behave, what sort of things you can do to impress the guy you have a crush on and various other tidbits of information that will help you navigate these initial meetings with success. Hopefully, you will gain some new insights that will allow you to make a better impression following your first encounter. Let's get into it.

RULE SIX

Hold On To Your Value

Your value as a woman is something you absolutely have to hold onto. For one thing, the way that men see you and treat you should not define or affect your perceived self-value whatsoever. This is the same for any human being and any other human interaction. If you base your own value upon what others think, you are always going to be at the mercy of external factors. Partly that is because everyone thinks other people look at them differently than they actually do. It is also partly because it is human nature to tear down other people to make yourself feel better. It takes a great deal of practice and empathy not to do that.

When it comes to attracting guys, they will know if you are willing to compromise your value as a woman or allow someone else to control it. It will be obvious to their subconscious mind even if they do not actually dwell upon it consciously. When you talk to a man and he senses doubt and insecurity, he is going to waver in his respect for you. It is even more pronounced when you say things that give the game away.

For example, many women fall into a trap where they feel insecure, and so they make comments trying to get their significant other to build up their confidence. Have you ever said this to someone: "I can tell you don't love me like you used to. I see how you looked at that woman last night." This is a dead giveaway to a guy that your value as a woman is diminishing in your own mind. When that happens, your value diminishes in his mind as well. Never make comments like this. Never assume that a date or significant other is more interested in other women than he is in you. Even if he looks at them intensely, you don't actually know what is going on in his head.

Besides, when a guy sees an attractive woman, he almost can't help but turn his head. That doesn't mean he is more interested in them or that he wants to monkey-branch away from you. Attraction is built on many things including looks, personality, sense of humor and much more. But what is not attractive is a woman who does not value herself in comparison with other women.

This is a trap women often fall into with celebrity crushes. Just about everyone out there has a celebrity crush. Celebrities are seen as almost a special brand of human being. They are put up on a pedestal due to their presence in our favorite films and on television shows, and it is completely within the bounds of human nature to feel attraction to them. But there are very few men out there who seriously consider that they have a chance to date a celebrity. Getting jealous because your boyfriend has a celebrity crush who he talks about will do nothing but make you look as if you are not confident enough to stand up against a fantasy.

The truth is, you are much more appealing and interesting to your boyfriend than a celebrity is. That's because you are attainable. But the more value that you can give yourself, the more you will be elevated in his eyes. While you may never attain the fantasy level of your boyfriend's celebrity crush, when it comes to the real world, you will be number one on his list of desirable women.

Every bit of value that you accumulate and make your own is value that is going to be yours innately for the rest of your life. You're the only one who can build your own value. You're also the only one who can take that value away. You may diminish your value because of comments that someone else has made or beliefs that you have about yourself that are driven by things that other people have done. However, you are still the only one who has the power to restore or remove value from your inner being. Don't allow other people to control whether or not you have value — own it and enhance it, and never let anyone diminish it.

RULE SEVEN

Let's Skip Discussions About Your Ex

One of the biggest pet peeves we guys have with women we date is that they continually talk about their exes. This is a complete mystery to us. We usually have no desire to talk about our ex-partners. We have usually long since moved on and, with you in our lives, we have no desire to think about our exes. Sure, we may consider them fleetingly from time to time, maybe even compare them to you subconsciously at first, but the fact is that whoever we are currently with is going to shine brighter in our minds than anyone from the past.

But, certainly in my experiences and those of my male friends, women seem to bring up their ex-boyfriends — a lot. There may be perfectly legitimate reasons for this. It may be some kind of defense mechanism or comparison tool that you use. It might be a tactic for you to provoke a jealous response in the guy you are dating. But you should know what guys think when you bring up your ex-partner.

It's very simple. We think if you bring up your

ex-boyfriend, you are obviously not over him.

If you have been dating your new partner for a while, then this might cause nothing more than an argument. However, it can kill a new relationship extremely fast. When you are in love with someone you will do almost anything to keep that relationship going. When you break up with that person, it takes a great deal of time to get over that relationship and move on to another one. You can rebound with someone temporarily, but there is a good chance that you will go back to your ex.

So, when you bring up your ex, especially during the first few dates, then guys can understandably assume that you are not really interested in them as someone to date for the long term. You are basically interested in a rebound date. In fact, it gives the impression you are looking for someone with whom you can lament about your broken relationship. This is a huge turnoff.

If you are not over your ex-boyfriend yet, then you should not be dating. You should wait until you are completely over him before you go out on dates. Guys are going to know when you are not really into them. They are going to be able to sense when the date is not going well and if that is because you are still hung up over your ex. You need to deal with that baggage before you begin dating again.

The reason for this is simple. We want to be the guy who sweeps you off your feet and makes you forget about all of those other guys from your past. It sounds arrogant, but we want to make you feel like we are superior to all those other guys in every way. Guys who are confident in themselves will believe that innately, unless you dash those illusions.

One thing that you definitely don't want to do is engage your new partner in any sort of comparison with your ex. Even if you evaluate fairly, you're going to dent their self-confidence and it will make it very difficult for your relationship to flourish. If they try to bring up the topic, simply steer the conversation in another direction and end it right there. Men can have fragile egos and nothing positive can come from this line of conversation.

Of course, if you follow the advice in this book, then you probably will not have to worry about dating guys who lack confidence. Even so, once you are in a new relationship with a nice guy, just make sure you avoid bringing up your ex.

RULE EIGHT

Pettiness Turns Us Off

Let's face it, some people — men and women — can be extremely petty. And I don't think you would shoot me if I suggested that some women judge each other a little harshly. The fact is, you seldom hear guys criticizing each other for the way they dress or the type of shoes they are wearing. Sure, some guys may brag that the basketball shoes they bought are way more expensive and prestigious than the ones their friend purchased, but guys don't purposely try to highlight small things such as mismatching clothes or someone putting on a little weight.

So why do some women feel compelled to engage in this behavior? When I looked into this subject, I actually found a couple of social science-backed theories. One of them had to do with the fact that women tend to take out aggression and stress in some way other than physically fighting. This apparently comes from an evolutionary need to protect the womb. Men sometimes take out stress, aggression and feelings of low self-worth through physical attack, while women often do it by non-physical routes.

The other theory states that in our evolutionary past, women competed fiercely for the strongest man in the tribe. Having the strongest man was a point of pride, but also meant you were likely to have strong and healthy offspring who could withstand the harsh living conditions and childhood diseases. It also often meant a much better social status within the tribe or village because it was the strongest man who became the chieftain or rose to other positions of power. Women came to regard being prized by strong men as their route to security and social elevation. This compelled them to battle fiercely with other women.

Interestingly, the theory also states that in some instances women are not actually competing with other women. Instead, they are competing with themselves, and directing their anger towards other women. This is a self-esteem issue. When you feel like you are not worth it, you can raise your own profile by taking down other women. You can see this tactic reflected in gossip, bad-mouthing and spreading rumors.

Now let's bring it back to the present day. What you need to understand is that men do not appreciate women being petty. When you go out with a guy to a bar and you comment on how another woman's dress makes her look fat or how she doesn't have the calves to wear those heels, it rings alarm bells regarding your nature. It also makes us question whether you're saying similar petty things about us behind our backs.

The bottom line to keep in mind here is that pettiness is a turnoff for a guy. Being petty about not being given enough ice in your drink or the bartender not serving you quickly enough will backfire. We don't want a woman to be petty. It makes her look selfish, self-absorbed and unattractive. Of course, the same is absolutely true of men.

If there is a legitimate complaint, then it is certainly within your rights to mention it, but if it is something really small, then most guys you are going out with are not going to be impressed by hearing about it.

RULE NINE

It's Ok To Show Gratitude

You should know that guys really like it when women show gratitude for the effort that they make on a date. Because of the chivalric code that has been around for hundreds of years, guys are generally expected to do everything from paying for the date to making the first move.

In this day and age, it is not actually the guy's sole responsibility to take care of everything. But that's not to say that some guys do not enjoy doing everything, including opening doors and doing all the other chivalrous stuff that men have been expected to do through the ages. In fact, many men take pride in this aspect. However, one of the things that men do not enjoy is being expected to do these things and being shown little or no gratitude for their effort.

That's why it is important to show gratitude when you are on a date with a guy who is being generous and respectful. If he opens the car door for you, do not just walk past him like you are the Queen of England and it is expected of him. The same thing goes for buying a round of drinks or picking up the tab for dinner. Let him know that you appreciate his efforts. This will build a better relationship as he is going to feel validated, and the positive feedback will make him enjoy being on the date with you more.

Showing gratitude costs you nothing. Men can spend a great deal of time planning out the perfect date, and if you act bored or ungrateful because not all of the activities on the date meet your expectations, it hurts our feelings and makes us not want to pursue the relationship.

As for finances, everybody has their own unique financial situation. It is impossible to know exactly how much effort it took for a guy to pay for the date until you get to know him and find out what he does for a living, the kind of bills he has and other financial information. But it doesn't matter if he is a millionaire or only makes minimum wage, it's common courtesy to show gratitude when he picks up the tab. This of course works both ways in a relationship.

So, to recap, please don't take it for granted when a guy takes you out on the town and buys you dinner, pays for movie tickets, buys you popcorn and soda and opens doors for you on dates. It costs nothing to be nice and it reaps remarkable rewards. You might find that a guy you didn't much like at first completely changes into a more confident and nicer person because you yourself came across as someone with a generous spirit. But guys are definitely turned off when you act like them paying for everything or doing all the work is simply what is expected.

RULE TEN

Avoid Getting Tipsy

Alcohol is an interesting substance. The first thing that is so interesting about it is that it affects everyone a little differently. For example, one person can have two or three beers and they feel a heavy buzz that makes them stagger or slur their speech. Another person might be able to drink an entire 12-pack of beer without ever showing signs that they are intoxicated. It can sometimes be a mystery why alcohol affects people so differently, but when you are consuming it on a date, you definitely want to be cautious.

You might also have noticed that people's personalities change when they become intoxicated. Some people become really silly and funny, while others become sullen and even violent. This is true with both men and women. In either case, people often give away too much information when they are drinking. This makes getting drunk a not-so-great idea for the first few dates that you go on with someone.

But even if you do not get full-blown drunk, and only a little tipsy, you might still be doing a disservice to yourself in the relationship. Consuming four or five glasses of wine on a first date, even if it's a crutch to calm your nerves, could easily make someone think that you have an alcohol dependency problem. But the key thing to watch for is a change in behavior. If you become a little tipsy and this affects your personality, then the guy that you are out with is going to notice.

That's not to say that there are no circumstances where you should consume alcohol or you should completely abstain. Many people find that they are much more relaxed and can reveal their true self after a drink or two, especially in a pressured environment. But there are a couple things to keep in mind. First, as mentioned, you do not want to cross the line from being relaxed and loosened up to getting tipsy. Not on a first date, at the very least.

Second, wine can be pretty expensive when ordered with a dinner. If your date orders a soda that costs three bucks and you order a glass of vintage wine that costs 50, he is going to notice. Depending upon his financial situation, it might not matter all that much to his pocketbook, but it is still going to register mentally.

When it comes to alcohol, you need to be aware

of how you act when you're drinking. If, after a couple of drinks, you find yourself more relaxed and able to talk with someone with more ease than before, then having a couple of drinks may not be a bad idea at all. However, try to follow the guy's lead when it comes to alcoholic drinks — particularly if they are expensive. You don't want a guy to think that you are an alcoholic or that you have no regard for his budget.

Truth be told, guys who want to see a woman get blind drunk on a first date are generally those who are only interested in a one-night stand. That's not the type of guy you are looking for. You are looking for a guy who wants a relationship. That means he will want to get to know *you* on the first date, rather than get to know the person you become under the influence of alcohol.

You will have to decide where the line is for you, specifically. If you know that you are going to an expensive restaurant where they charge a fortune for drinks, then consider either offering to pay for the drinks yourself, going Dutch or having a drink before you leave your house to take the edge off. Of course, it might be a good idea to brush your teeth and chew some gum so that the guy who picks you up does not realize that you have had a drink before the date even started!

While one or two drinks may warm you up and even turn you into a better date, getting too tipsy on a date can be a turnoff. This will largely depend upon the guy and what his attitude is to drinking, but for most guys, they do not want a woman who drinks too much on the first few dates. It's a red flag. A genuine guy will want to get to know the real you without the influence of alcohol masking the picture. They also may not want to pay for very expensive drinks until a later date. Keep all these things in mind if you are looking to attract the right guy.

RULE ELEVEN

Date One Guy At A Time

Something else you might not be aware of is that guys dislike it when you are dating multiple people at the same time. Think of dating sort of like submitting a novel you have written to a carefully selected literary agent. Once you go through the selection process and have chosen the perfect literary agent who represents the genre of book that you've written, has represented some of your favorite authors in that genre and is willing to take your submission, it makes no sense to then go and submit it to 10 other agents at the same time. Instead, you want to wait until you've heard back from the first agent you carefully selected before you try your luck with a different one.

The same holds true for guys and dating multiple men at the same time. We don't want to feel like one of the pack. We don't want to feel like we are competing against a group of other guys on various dates that we know nothing about. You could have met the guy of your dreams on any of those other dates and we would never know. You could just be going through the motions with us because you already committed to our date.

Some guys in this situation feel like you are just stringing them along for dinner and drinks for as long as possible until you decide to take the next step and start dating that other guy of your dreams.

I know that is a harsh assessment. But friends of mine have confided in taking this view on more than one occasion.

To offer some flexibility, this exclusivity can be applied after, say, the second date. When you go out on a first or even second date with someone you can be forgiven for making arrangements with other potential suitors. This is simply being pragmatic and efficient. But after two dates, you should know whether you want to keep dating them or not. If you have been dating someone else for a long time, guys generally don't want to be on a date with you. It's just plain weird.

There are actually quite a few reasons why you might want to avoid dating multiple guys at the same time. The first is obviously the one that this chapter is based around: none of the guys you are dating are going to be pleased to find out that there are others you are juggling as well. We just do not like that much competition, especially from someone who you have been dating for a while. But there are quite a few other reasons that you might want to consider.

When you are dating multiple people, it can be difficult to evaluate them fairly. You are always comparing one to the other in various areas, and it might not be fair to make these judgments, as everyone has their unique circumstances. Also, instead of focusing on a single relationship, you are focusing on several, and that makes it difficult to build on any of those relationships. When you are dating multiple people, there is a danger that these relationships stagnate rather than grow as you are not focused or invested in one thing.

Finally, things get confusing when you're dating multiple people. You might not remember who took you out for ice cream last Friday night and mentioning it in passing could get you in trouble with whoever you are currently on a date with! You might even call somebody by someone else's name. This gets especially complicated if you begin sleeping with one or more of the people you are seeing!

But even more than that, if a guy knows he's not the sole focus of your attention, he is not going to have much interest and energy invested into the relationship. This is because he knows that you are not available to be fully committed to him.

After all, why spend the maximum amount of energy trying to charm a woman who is probably going to choose someone else?

Focus on dating a single person at a time. You will usually be able to tell after two or three dates whether he is the right person for you. There may be a lack of chemistry between you when you're together. There may be personality conflicts. You may find that even though you were initially attracted to the person, his dimples are no longer cute or his strange habits not so endearing.

If your goal is to build something meaningful, then you are going to have to give a relationship a chance. If you are fairly selective about the guys you date, then whenever you go out with them it should be a quality experience. You will be able to get a much clearer picture of what life would be like with them in the future and determine just how far you want to pursue dating them.

It's perfectly okay to be picky when it comes to choosing who you want to go on a date with and who you want to say yes to for a second date. Just stick to a single person after the second date, as a general rule. Trust me, guys will appreciate it when you do.

RULE TWELVE

We Like The Natural Look — For Real

One of the things that guys often say is that they like it when a woman does not wear any makeup. But it seems that no woman in history has ever believed their significant other when he has said this. That's because men and women regard makeup very differently. Some women regard makeup as a necessity that sets their face in order and makes them presentable for the day. Men regard makeup as an accessory that is not always needed, but sometimes looks nice.

So, when some women go without makeup, they feel as if they are missing a vital part of themselves. They feel as if they are not able to present themselves in public, and especially avoid things like having pictures taken that could end up on social media. Some women would no sooner go out without makeup on as they would go barefoot to a restaurant or visit the grocery store in their underwear. To them, makeup is a necessity and an integral part of their day.

The problem with this is that it can show a decided lack of self-esteem. If you think that you cannot look beautiful without makeup, then you are mistaken. When a guy tells you that he prefers you without makeup or that he thinks you look beautiful with or without it, he isn't just being flattering. He truly thinks that you look good with or without makeup!

Remember, self-confidence is a must in making sure that guys are attracted to you. Guys want women who believe in themselves. There is nothing sexier than a woman who knows who she is and has the confidence, poise and attitude to back that up. When you refuse to go out in public without makeup, or you use too much makeup to compensate for some imaginary flaws, it signals you lack self-confidence.

So, should you go out into the public eye without your makeup on? Should you allow yourself to be photographed and videoed without makeup? That is something that is totally up to you, but if you have been paying attention to recent celebrity trends, you might have noticed that there is a growing list of celebrities who have had photo shoots without any makeup on and had those pictures published online or in a major magazine. Instagram is full of celebrities with "nude" faces.

This has to do with the recent movements to

empower women. For example, companies using normal-size women instead of super-thin supermodels to show their clothing, and all of the other empowerment actions that are being taken by women all over the world. This is a great thing, and for a guy who is not threatened by self-assured women, it is actually a huge attraction. Women who are confident enough in themselves to go out in public without any makeup on or who do not have to conform to body-shape ideals that they see in magazines are actually incredibly sexy to enlightened guys.

There are still going to be guys out there who look at women with the supermodel filter and refuse to date them unless they are thin almost to the point of being unhealthy and caked with makeup — but those are not the kinds of guys who you want anyway. I'm sure the kind of guy you want believes in empowering women and thinks that every woman out there is beautiful in her own way no matter what size and shape she is or what makeup she happens to be wearing (or not wearing).

The key takeaway here is that you should be open to believing guys when they tell you they prefer you without makeup. Believe me, if a guy says that to you, then he, at least in most cases, really means it. The losers out there who think you are too plain unless you are caked with makeup are not going to tell you this. They are going to be reluctant to take you out and show you off as arm candy unless you have the right makeup and clothes on. That's not what you're looking for.

RULE THIRTEEN

Pitch In For The Bill

One thing that you might not realize is just how much it is appreciated whenever a woman offers to help out with the bill when it arrives. Guys who take women out to fancy restaurants are usually trying to impress them. While that is definitely nice, you can impress the guy right back by offering to split the bill with him. He may or may not take you up on the offer, but he is going to remember the gesture and mark it down as a positive character trait.

Even in this day and age, some women believe that they are entitled to a free pass when they are asked out on a date. They somehow believe that they can choose any sort of activity to do on a date and the guy should be expected to pay for it.

To understand why this is the case, you have to look back in history. In the past, it was expected that men would pick up the check because women rarely worked. For example, throughout the early and mid-20thcentury, women were usually not employed, except during those rare occasions when women had to bulk up the workforce because men were at war.

So, it was expected that men would do everything when they went on dates with women. They would drive the car because it was mostly men who owned the cars. They would pay for the meal or the movie or whatever activity they were doing because they had the jobs. They would also be responsible for buying the engagement ring when it came time to propose. In those days, it would have been unheard of for a woman to propose to a man.

That recent history has shaped the way that dating is conducted today. But circumstances have changed. While it is true that, in general, women still get paid less than men, there are major efforts to change this and to promote equality across the genders. What is not true anymore is that women are solely the ones who stay at home and men are the ones who go to work. These days, couples almost always both work. This is due to advances such as maternity leave and also the rising cost of living, which requires both partners to have jobs. In addition, the job of stay-at-home parent is well on its way to being divided equally between men and women.

So, while the financial situation of men and women has changed drastically, with many women even earning more than the men they go on dates with, men are still generally expected to pick up the tab. This can turn into a major financial burden if someone on a minimum wage job starts dating someone with expensive tastes! Of course, such situations are rare, but the point is that for guys, being asked to split the bill is a much-appreciated gesture.

Even if a guy isn't going to have to rack up credit card debt in order to pay for a meal, he is still going to appreciate it when you offer to contribute financially to the date in some way or another. This lets him know that you appreciate his efforts and the fact that he has picked up the bill on previous dates, or is willing to pick up the bill on this date. Some guys will not even entertain allowing their date to contribute financially, but that does not mean they do not appreciate being asked.

You can also do things like offering to pick up a round of drinks when the two of you go out with some of his buddies. This is definitely impressive, and you will not only rise in value in his eyes, but his friends will boost your standing by saying positive things to him. So, the next time you go out, just offer to help out a little bit. It is one of the best things you can do to improve your relationship with a guy that you like.

PART THREE

The Thrill Of The Chase

The chase is one of the key parts of healthy human relationships. A lot of people do not like the chase stage because they are not very good at playing the game. Unfortunately, just because you are bad at the game doesn't mean that you get a free pass on attracting someone. The fact is that everyone has to play the chase game to an extent in order to enter into a healthy relationship. But why is this the case?

It starts with looking all the way back to the evolutionary past of humans. The chase was necessary, because it singled out the strongest of the tribe. Back then, the chase was literally a real thing, a competition where men would compete for a woman and women would compete for a man. The most desirable and strong men secured the most desirable women because that's how natural selection works.

In today's society, you still have to compete for the man that you want. If you have a crush on someone, you are competing with other women for that man. They may not be actively pursuing him now, but they could be in future if he shows an interest. That means it is up to you to get him interested in you instead. So how do you do that?

That's exactly where the chase comes in. In order to get someone interested in you, you first have to pique their interest, and then you have to make them think that they have a chance of losing you. So, the first date is more important than just about anything else when it comes to the chase. If you can get someone very interested in you on the first date, and then play hard to get for the next few dates, they are going to focus their attention on you rather than the woman who is readily available and offering herself to him. That, paradoxically, is how the psychology of the chase works.

That's where many women run into a problem. They think that by being available at all times that the man they like will choose them. But men like a competition. More importantly, they hate losing out on something that they would have really loved. When you play hard to get, it gets your man focused and interested. He doesn't want to lose out — it's in his nature — so he is going to pursue you; if you can get him to chase you for long enough, then the odds are stacked in your favor.

The chapters in this section are all about the chase. You will learn techniques on how to keep a man interested after that initial first date. You will learn what the purpose of the chase is and why it is so important. You will also learn some techniques that keep a man pursuing you and avoid you overplaying your hand. Let's get started.

RULE FOURTEEN

Don't Be Too Available

One of the things that women can sometimes do to dull a relationship is to make themselves too available. There are several reasons why you don't want to make yourself too available to the guy who you have been seeing. For one thing, you want him to realize that you have your own life and that he is just a part of it and not the sole focus of it. This is something that any decent guy will appreciate. He will realize, without you saying so, that you are busy with work, hobbies, friends and family, and that sometimes you will only have a limited time to spend with him.

Another reason why you shouldn't make yourself too available — sometimes even when you actually are available — is due to the fact that any guy who is interested in you will become *more* interested in you when he cannot always get a hold of you right away. That's because of the jealousy factor. No matter how confident a guy is, if he likes a woman and she is not available right away, his mind might ponder what she could be doing — and with whom. Of course, this will make him even more curious and interested. It's a puzzle to solve.

Now, there is a distinction here between guys thinking that you might be seeing other people and *knowing* that you are dating other people. When you are dating someone, even if it is the first date, it is best not to mention that you are going out with a few other people. The truth is that guys want you to be dating just them. That might be unrealistic of course so, as guys, we will settle for just not knowing that you are dating other people for the first couple of dates. However, if you continually go out on dates with us and are still dating other people, then that turns into a problem. This is different to a guy *speculating* that you're out with other guys. The former is most definitively negative while the latter can create pangs of jealousy, which can actually improve your relationship.

So, how do you perfect this balance of not being too unavailable but not being too available either?

When he calls, don't always answer the phone. Not very many people call on the phone these days anyway, but if he is the type of guy who likes to call you, especially after sending a text, then just ignore his phone call and text him back later. If he texts you, sometimes take a little time to get back to him.

The thrill of the chase is an important part of a relationship. Of course, you don't want to take it too far. You don't want to make him feel like he is chasing after you with no chance of success. In fact, you always want to leave him feeling like he is just on the verge of catching up with you. This can be a very difficult balance to achieve, especially if you are not used to leading the chase. Many women find that they are the ones usually doing the chasing, and being the person being chased is a different role to get used to.

Not being available all the time is an important part of building desirability. As your relationship becomes closer, this will become more natural over time and you won't have to fake it anymore.

The main thing to keep in mind here is that you do not want to be sitting around waiting for your phone to ring or for your next text to come in. You don't want to be constantly refreshing your email to see if he has sent a message. You definitely don't want to respond the very second he contacts you, because that will just show him he is in charge, and it will make him lose a little bit of interest in you.

Along with this, make sure that you do not sleep with your dates too early (more on this later). In fact, put this off as long as you possibly can. You should definitely never sleep with someone on the first five dates. Even though guys are generally always interested in sex, the good guys will respect women who make them wait. The longer that you can make him chase you and avoid that ultimate physical commitment, the more chance there is for strong feelings to blossom.

RULE FIFTEEN

Respect The Chase

The chase is an important part of building any relationship. It refers to the pursuit of a romantic interest while the other person (the person being pursued) attempts to draw out the pursuit as much as possible. In a healthy relationship, this should go both ways. One person should pursue the other, and then there is an arbitrary switch where the person doing the pursuing gets pursued. What this means is that both parties are interested in the other person, but have gained enough experience with human relationships to know that, sometimes, when you give someone exactly what they want too soon, they no longer want it so much.

In some relationships, one party will exclusively pursue the other. There is no back and forth, there is only the woman chasing after the man or the man chasing after the woman. This can also result in healthy relationships, as long as the person being pursued finds value in the relationship with the person doing the pursuing.

Ideally, you want to be the person being pursued. So, your job is to draw out the chase as long as possible, but you also want to make sure that you don't push it.

You also want to be careful. Coming on too strong in the beginning is something that people with low self-confidence and little experience in relationships often do. When you are attracted to someone, your body is experiencing all sorts of new feelings and sensations: hormones are being released and it can be difficult to sort out your emotions. That's why many people fall into the trap of coming on too strong to the person they are attracted to. The problem is, this can be a little overwhelming for the other person. In other words, if the chase is too easy, then they are not going to be that interested. Again, it's about the psychology of the chase.

No one really knows why human relationships work this way. It likely has something to do with the way that our brains evolved throughout the millennia as we evolved from male predators who chased down the females we wanted to mate with, and from females on the lookout for the strongest, most powerful mate to secure. Obviously, we no longer need to pursue relationships in this primitive way. But somehow, our brains, our libido and sexual drives all require the chase to heighten our interest in the other person.

So, how do you keep the chase going without pushing it too far?

As I have previously stated, one of the ways in which this can be done is by being unavailable part of the time. If your crush calls you on the phone, don't pick up on the first ring and don't always be available for a date. Make him work a little for it. Lots of couples that have been together for decades tell the story of the man asking out the woman multiple times before she finally relented and said yes. They lived happily ever after beyond that initial chase.

You can also make the chase last longer by not giving away your emotions too soon. Again, make him work for your affections. Make him feel at one time that you are really into him and then have him wonder all night what something you said meant. Remember, this is only at first. You don't want to do this for very long. As your relationship starts to deepen, you will want to move onto the next stage. You should also avoid sleeping with the person you are interested in for a least a few dates. The longer you can draw it out, and create mystery and excitement in the relationship, the more chance you will have of developing a long-term union.

But don't push it too far. Waiting days to get

back to someone doesn't demonstrate that you might be interested, it demonstrates that you don't care enough about them to get back to them within a reasonable amount of time. A reasonable amount of time means that if he texts you in the morning, waiting until the afternoon should be about the maximum time that you should keep him sweating. Just use your common sense and be sure that you're not pushing him away while you are trying to attract him.

RULE SIXTEEN

Beware Mixed Signals On Sex

In the previous two chapters we discussed the thrill of the chase. Gently playing the game and making a guy wonder if you are really interested in him can actually contribute to a healthy pursuit. But there is one bit of advice that bears repeating: don't sleep with your crush too early. However, this can get a little confusing because it makes it sound as if you should play the game with sex as well. I want to be clear that this is not a good idea.

Sex is a wonderful thing. It can be used as a reward, but it can also be used as a weapon. Sex can be withheld from a significant other in retaliation for some offense. When you are first dating someone, you don't want to send mixed signals about sex. You want to make sure that he knows you are not going to give it up in the first few dates. You don't want to give him a certain date that you would be willing to sleep with him by, because then you won't be able to weed out guys who are only looking for a hook-up and will give up after that time. However, you do want to state: "I don't sleep with someone until I've gotten to know them really well."

There is a major difference between having casual sex with someone who you are interested in but not necessarily for the long-term, and sleeping with someone you are actually cultivating a relationship with. There is a deeper level that you move into after you've slept with someone. There is much more of a commitment to each other, as there is a sharing of intimacy. When you sleep with someone you are interested in dating long-term, you want it to be something special. You want them to remember it for a long time and you want to look back on it as special.

Another bit of advice that goes along with this is to try not to get drunk with the person that you're interested in dating long-term. Even if you have been on three or four dates, you still want to avoid getting really drunk. For one thing, you may forget the chase altogether and come on too strong and set your relationship back. But the main thing is that there is a danger of sleeping with someone after you have both drank a lot. The negative thing about this is that one or both of you may not remember the actual sex in the morning. This is something that you want to avoid if you are building a relationship. Each step you take is a building block that you are putting into place. The sex factor is a big one, and it is a defining moment in a relationship.

You might be wondering when you'll know it is the right time to have sex with someone you are interested in. This is difficult to pin down, but it will generally be after several dates, a few shared kisses and a few nights where you came close to sleeping with them. You want to make sure they know you are not trying to lead them on or withholding sex from them for the sake of it, but that you are following your original guidelines that you set down when you entered the relationship.

One way that you can manage the sex without sending mixed signals or leading them on is by allowing it in stages. For example, after a couple of dates, allow them to give you a chaste kiss outside of your home. From there, you might have a short make-out session. You can use your imagination and determine where you might go from there!

So make sure you are clear and upfront about sex, even while you are participating in the rituals of a relationship such as playing hard to get. There is nothing wrong with subtly making your partner wonder whether or not you are interested in them, but don't lead him on about sex because it could backfire on you. This is one topic in your relationship that you want to be upfront and clear about.

PART FOUR

Understanding Male Behavior

I'll be the first to admit, we guys can sometimes exhibit some pretty strange behavior. We sulk, we withdraw, we have been known to check out other women right in front of you and we do all sorts of things that we know you are not too keen on. But what you need to understand is that there is a reason for almost all of this behavior, and understanding these reasons will go a long way towards understanding us better.

In this section, we will be examining some of the behaviors often exhibited by guys that women find difficult to understand. What you should take away from this is that if you like a guy, and he exhibits some of these behaviors, it doesn't necessarily mean he doesn't like you or doesn't respect you. Many of the behaviors listed here are so deeply ingrained in male brains that it can take a lot of effort to change.

For example, did you know that behavioral

scientists have theorized that there are evolutionary reasons why men look at other women when they pass by, even when you are sitting right next to us? This is not an action that men do to be jerks. This is something they do because, well, they are men, and whether it makes us jerks or not, we are likely to still exhibit these behaviors.

So, we will be covering a few of the more annoying behaviors that you have probably noticed with guys in the past. When you are dating someone, you have to keep in mind that the female brain works completely differently than the male brain. There is a reason for each and every behavior that we exhibit, and you may not be able to understand these reasons because of the perspective from which you view them.

The important thing to keep in mind here is that these are automatic behaviors. They are innate actions that are encoded into our genes that are mostly out of our control without a great deal of practice and time. I'm not saying a guy should be able to treat you badly and without respect, and that you have to simply accept it as "a part of their nature". There is never an excuse for that. However, men have a propensity to display certain actions from time to time which you may find confusing and bewildering.

You have probably heard women talk about how they have to train their men. Well, unfortunately for us, this is actually closer to the truth than is comfortable! We do have to train ourselves to stop certain behaviors and instead exhibit others so that we can maintain harmony in a relationship.

Let's delve in.

RULE SEVENTEEN

Understanding The Zone Out

Okay, so every guy has been here. We're sitting on the couch or laying in bed and we start thinking about something. We basically go silent while we intensely contemplate whatever it is that is on our mind. At this point, women often are curious and start asking questions about what is preoccupying us. This withdrawal into our own world could even be seen as rude, selfish or plain bad manners.

You see, we could be thinking about a million different things. We might be thinking about sports or what's on television later. We might be considering a strategy for an online gaming session or replaying a poker hand which we should have played differently. We might be thinking about the future or just about any other topic. It doesn't really mean anything about the relationship when we zone out in this way. This is something guys do from time to time and, if there are no major problems with your relationship currently, you shouldn't be worried about it.

Of course, there are instances where guys are

zoning out and not paying attention to you for reasons that you should be concerned about. He might be contemplating the relationship. It may have gotten more serious than he intended and he's evaluating how he feels about that. He might be wondering how he can make a dignified exit. However, it is important to keep in mind that these specific instances are pretty rare and are usually accompanied by other major signs that there is trouble in your relationship.

If you have a good relationship and the guy suddenly zones out on the couch for no reason, it could really be nothing more than him making plans for later in the day or wondering what his next meal will be.

But what about when you are trying to talk to him and he zones out on you? This is another issue altogether, but not one that you should be overly concerned about. The first thing that you have to understand is that women are naturally better listeners than men. Men are more focused on action. They are not so much into discussing an issue unless they are in a position to take action on it.

To demonstrate how different men and women are when it comes to listening, consider this scenario:

A woman has just found out that she is going to lose her job at the end of the month. Her friends come over and give her hugs and discuss with her how it is going to affect her family life, and they let her know how much they support her. They may spend an entire evening just comforting her and finding out what her feelings are about the job ending.

If you put men in that exact same scenario, generally their feelings, beyond the initial shock, will be put on the back burner. Their male friends, while offering sympathy, will likely come up with practical suggestions to secure another job. They would immediately want to take action, scouring the newspapers, Craigslist and anywhere else they can look for a new job. They will spend little time finding out how he feels about the job ending or trying to comfort him. That's just not how guys are. While there are exceptions, we're not natural listeners.

Of course, as men, we know that women need to talk and share their feelings. We also know that you want us to listen, and we will make the best effort we can. When we love someone and want to make a relationship work, we are certainly willing to change some of our innate behaviors in order to be compatible with yours. But you have to understand that when we do zone out, it has nothing to do with you or what you are saying. We are not purposely trying to insult you or antagonize you by zoning out, but instead we occasionally do what comes naturally to us. Hopefully, now that you have this information, you will be a little more understanding when your guy suddenly seems to go blank for no apparent reason.

RULE EIGHTEEN

We Check Out Other Women

Okay, so there is something that we men do that drives women absolutely crazy. And really, you cannot be blamed for hitting the roof when it happens. In fact, we know that this action is likely to land us in trouble and, even though we don't want to hurt you, we still do it from time to time. It is impossible to prevent it from happening 100 percent of the time.

It is when we look at other women.

So, you're sitting in a coffee shop having a quiet drink with your boyfriend or a guy you have started dating, and you notice to your horror that an attractive woman in a skin-tight dress has just walked by and your man cannot take his eyes off her. After a minute, he pulls his eyes away and looks back at you and sees that you are, let's say, annoyed. He gives you an embarrassed smile but doesn't seem to care all that much just how much he has disrespected you. So, what's going on? Why did he do that? Are all men totally insensitive jerks? The answer is no.

The truth is, looking at attractive women is a kind of reflex action for men. There is some science behind this statement. Looking at attractive women when we were teenagers released brain chemicals that made us feel good — namely dopamine and serotonin. That's just how puberty works. Those same neurological pathways are there to a certain degree in adulthood, although not quite as strong as they used to be, and so it can be considered natural (though no doubt bad manners!) to look at attractive women. The science says that men are subconsciously assessing women as mating options and looking for health cues such as facial symmetry and hip-to-waist ratio for childbearing.

Now, this doesn't necessarily mean that you will have to live with this primal behavior for your entire life. We understand that it hurts you. We understand that it makes you feel jealous but, to an extent at least, we are not doing it on purpose. A decent guy certainly will attempt to avoid looking at other women when out with his significant other. We will try to control this propensity so that we do not hurt the woman we are with.

Unfortunately, this is a continual struggle. It is not just a psychological remnant from our teenage years, it is also a behavior constantly being reinforced every time we watch television, read a magazine or view an online video. When advertisers want men to pay attention to something, they use attractive women. Think of all the beer commercials that you've seen. How many of them featured attractive women? Advertisers know this is something men struggle with, and therefore they try to stimulate that chemical release mechanism with attractive women — usually wearing as little clothing as possible. They want the attractive woman to release the happy hormones which are then linked to the product. The theory being that the guy will now come to associate the product and its branding with warm and fuzzy feelings of arousal, which will in turn drive sales. It may seem crude, but it works.

Exploiting this compulsion to seek out beauty and virility is even present in television shows. *Game of Thrones* was a wildly popular television show on HBO. It was based on a series of fantasy books. However, unlike the books, the TV series was full of naked women. Would the TV show have been just as popular without the nudity? Perhaps. But the series producers knew that adding lashings of nudity to the narrative would be a surefire way to win the enthusiasm of the core demographic for epic fantasy: middle-aged men.

Men are continually fighting this urge in the presence of women. Understanding the mechanisms behind this behavior will hopefully go some way towards diffusing your anger when your man occasionally does a double-take to briefly look at another woman. If it's not gratuitous and you otherwise trust him not to stray from your relationship, then it might be a good strategy to not immediately fly off the handle. You have every right to make your displeasure known and it is only by receiving feedback from you that he can alter his future behavior. However, try to appreciate that he is not intentionally trying to hurt you, and he is not looking for an option to cheat.

Good men who care about the women they are with will do whatever they can to adjust their behavior. It is more difficult to do when they are young but, as we become more mature over the years, we look less and less at other women — no matter how attractive they are! Of course, that doesn't mean it will never happen. The key takeaway is that it doesn't represent a threat to you or your relationship. It doesn't mean that your man loves you less or thinks you are less attractive.

RULE NINETEEN

A Period Drama

One of the things that probably makes you quite angry is when we blame your behavior on premenstrual syndrome or PMS. While I'm not saying that this behavior is right or excusable, you should at least understand where your guy is coming from and why he might say it. Smart guys learn never to do it, but it may take a while until that happens. Still, it is a good idea to see things from our perspective and understand why we think that your behavior could be blamed on hormonal imbalances caused by premenstrual syndrome.

The first thing you have to understand is that not everything you ladies do is always rational — and the same is perfectly true of men. We might tell you something one day and you laugh or seem happy to hear it, and then get angry when we say the exact same thing a few days later. It can sometimes be impossible to predict what your behavior or mood is going to be. Are you going to react to a joke the same way you did the last time you heard it? Do we need to avoid certain conversation topics always, or only during a certain time of the month? These are all questions that guys have had to consider through experience.

You have to understand that we mostly don't get PMS beyond the theoretical. We know that it happens once a month and that you are uncomfortable during these times, but most guys have no idea what the scope and breadth of PMS actually is. For anyone who has actually taken the time to learn what their significant other might be going through hormonally and emotionally, the results are eye-opening. If guys really knew what sorts of things you endure when you experience premenstrual symptoms, we would never make jokes about it again.

But since most guys never bother to investigate PMS, it generally remains a mystery to them; the symptoms that you experience, the cramps, the pain and misery that you feel is all abstract. It is something that we hear you say, but it is not something that we actually understand. We have nothing to compare it to, no frame of reference in our own lives. There is no process in the male anatomy that compares to it. It is like you trying to understand how it feels to be kicked in the testicles. On one level, you can see how it would be painful, but you will never understand the depth of the pain that we feel when that happens.

Having said that, if men were to experience getting kicked in the lower region once a month at the same time that women experienced premenstrual symptoms, then there might be some basis for comparison and we might stop joking about it. But since, joking aside, we have nothing to compare it to directly, you might offer a little leniency when it comes to judging your man for joking about your PMS.

There are things that you can do to improve the situation, of course. The first thing is to sit down with your man and explain exactly, in as explicit detail as possible, what it is you go through when you experience PMS. You want to explain how bad the cramps get, how you feel miserable, how it affects your mental health and your state of mind while this is going on. In addition, explain how much of an inconvenience it is to have to deal with bleeding and ensuring that you always have access to tampons or pads.

The psychological aspect is very important to get across for a healthier, more nurturing relationship. The mood swings are a phenomenon that we find hard to understand. We understand having pain, and how certain conditions can make you more uncomfortable than others. For example, we understand that ailments such as an impacted or abscessed tooth can be extremely painful and put you out of the running for just about any activity. We get pain. But what we don't understand are the hormonal changes involved with PMS. That's the reason why most guys will joke about PMS, because they do not understand why their wives or significant others act the way that they do. Terms such as estrogen and progesterone are generally alien to us.

Since men do not experience these hormonal changes the same way, the only thing that you can really do is try to describe it to them. One comparison that men have for these kinds of hormonal changes is what it was like to go through puberty. Going through puberty was a difficult and sometimes uncomfortable process for most people, and men who remember that stage of their life may have more sympathy.

But if your man does make jokes about PMS, try to understand that it isn't always personal. He just doesn't understand what you are going through. On a theoretical level, he understands the PMS is uncomfortable and that you are miserable, but it doesn't register at a gut level. So try to be a little lenient and educate him so, in the future, he knows that PMS is not something that he can use as a weapon whenever you may be emotional or sharp with him.

RULE TWENTY

We Are Committed To Numero Uno First

A key thing that you need to understand about men is that we commit to ourselves above everything and everyone else. That's not to say that in extreme circumstances we wouldn't sacrifice ourselves for our loved ones. But those kinds of life-and-death situations are extremely rare.

When we are first dating someone, we are committed to ourselves more than anything else. One of the biggest complaints that women have about men is that they refuse to commit. They just won't commit to marriage or a long-term relationship or moving up to the next level. You have to understand that our first commitment is to ourselves — to numero uno.

Whether or not it makes sense, men are often brought up to believe that life hinges on self-fulfillment. This means that when we think about happiness, we think about happiness in terms of ourselves. We think about what we can do to improve our own happiness and what life will be like in the future if we are able to achieve our goals. We do not really concern ourselves with goals that involve other people, because other people are unpredictable. We do not know how someone else may impact our goals — will they aid us or slow us down?

At first glance, to the average man, relationships are seen through the lens of achieving our goals and self-fulfillment. When we meet someone who we are attracted to, one of the first considerations we have is whether or not they will keep us from reaching our aims in life. This is different for men and women. Women often think about happiness in terms of other people. They incorporate other people into their life goals. They are comfortable with thinking about happiness in terms of an uncertain future as long as it includes people who are dear to them — including a romantic partner.

But that is different for guys. For us, we have to know specifically what a person is thinking and how they see their future before we can incorporate them into our plans. Our pragmatic mindset does not deal well with unpredictability. Relationships make us nervous when it comes to the pursuit of fulfillment and self-realization. Relationships are unpredictable and, let's face it, most romantic partnerships will end or fizzle out. We understand this on a theoretical level, even if we have not been in very many relationships beforehand.

So, how can you accommodate this?

When you get into a relationship with a guy, and he is looking at you as a potential interruption in his life rather than a reward, there may not be much that you can do about it. The best thing that you can do for yourself is to be honest with him about how you see your future. Discuss your life goals with him to see if there is alignment there. If there is, then the relationship can truly flourish as you then become a partner and facilitator of his own self-fulfillment. However, if there is no shared vision of the future, then it is unlikely that the union will succeed. In which case you can save yourself some time and move on to someone who you are more in tune with.

RULE TWENTY ONE

Why We Are Brutally Honest

One thing that often drives women crazy is how tactless men are. Rather than approaching a subject from the direction that you think we should, or bringing it up carefully or sensitively, we basically plunge right in without much thought as to how a person might feel because of our actions. We do this not only in our relationships with women, but also our relationships with other men. We are blunt and honest when it comes to certain things. But you have to understand that the reason we are brutally honest sometimes is due to the fact that we care so much.

That's what many women do not understand about men. They see us being too honest about certain subjects, and they make a judgment that we are basically insensitive brutes who have no feelings. That is not necessarily the case. While there are men out there who will make comments and be insensitive, not all men are like this. In fact, most men are actually quite sensitive to your feelings and do not want to hurt you. However, that does not mean that we are going to spare your feelings if we think that there is something that you need to know.

There was a recent video on YouTube from a couple that films various challenges and pranks on each other. One of the pranks they filmed was of the woman putting on too much makeup, making her look quite bizarre, and then seeing if her boyfriend would call her out on it. If you watch the video, you will notice that the boyfriend first tries to be supportive, and then cannot help himself and begins to tell her that her makeup looks horrible. She pretends to be upset about it, but eventually tells him that it was a prank and that she put the bad makeup on her face on purpose.

This is a good example of how many men think and act. If we feel there is something that you need to know, then we are most likely going to tell you to your face — in a fairly blunt manner. We think it is more efficient and effective for us to be perfectly blunt with you than it is for us to spare your feelings. This holds true whether we are telling you something about our relationship, whether we are offering an opinion on you how you look or any other situation where, to us, complete honesty seems the best policy.

So, the next time you notice your significant other being completely honest with you (tactless might be a better word!), it's worth bearing in mind that he is probably not on a mission to cause you as much distress as possible. It's more likely that he isn't equipped with any other strategy to deliver the message. Here's where a frank discussion about future tactics might be good idea.

RULE TWENTY TWO

Make Us Feel Like Winners

Men need to feel like winners in their journey through life. We not only like to feel as though we are winning, but we also like to feel as though we are leading the competition. That's why this whole concept of the chase, which I explained previously, is so suited to the male mind. When you allow us to feel like we have a better chance with you than the other suitors pursuing you, it releases pleasure hormones and stokes positive emotions. Men want to feel like winners, and when they do they behave differently.

So what's the basis of all this? In the past, we had to come out on top or we would not have survived the evolutionary process. Natural selection says that only the strong survive, and men still have that deeply ingrained into their psyche. The way that men and women interacted and behaved in their evolutionary past is still the cause of a lot of the rituals and behaviors in the current dating game.

If you were to look at it from an outside perspective, you might think that these gender interactions were slightly crazy. After all, some of our dating behaviors don't seem to make much sense. We play hard to get when we're interested in someone. Then, sometimes, when we are actually with that person, we decide they are no longer interesting and the thrill of the chase is gone. This can happen after a short chase or an extremely long one. It's not always rational.

But many of our behaviors are rooted in our evolutionary past, and one of those that we have cultivated as men is winning. We have a need to feel like we are winning. We must feel like our actions are having a positive impact on our lives. Women might have several indicators of happiness that they can rely upon, but for men, winning is one of the best indicators of fulfillment. If we know that we are winning then we are ahead of the competition and we are the ones that are reaping the rewards.

This extends into all parts of our lives, including winning at work, winning at making you happy and completing our stated missions (whatever they happen to be). While you may be dropping hints that you think will make your man change certain aspects of his behavior, as long as he feels that he is winning with you, he is unlikely to notice any of those cues. Women often get annoyed because their man does not pick up on these hints. But you have to avoid setting him up to fail. Just tell him. Be totally honest with him. Don't beat around the bush, don't drop vague clues. Tell him up front and straight up, so that he can make the necessary adjustments and get back to winning with you once again. If a man feels like he cannot win in a relationship, which means making you happy, then he is not going to want to be in that relationship.

RULE TWENTY THREE

We're Not Trying To Hurt You

You can be forgiven for thinking from time to time that your man is purposely trying to hurt you with his behavior. Women take this personally, and they often complain to their friends that their man is acting in a certain way intentionally. While there are men out there who may actually be purposely trying to make you feel bad with their behavior, most men are not like that. The truth is, most men have little idea that the behavior they are exhibiting has a negative effect on the woman they like. You have to keep this in mind when it comes to dating.

The fact is that men's and women's brains work differently. While women may think about the consequences of their actions in terms of how it affects other people, men have more of a blind spot in this area. They often do not think about how a decision will impact others. They are thinking about themselves, because that is often how they were raised and what comes more naturally to the male brain. Men were taught to think about number one first, and then consider other people's feelings second. When this happens, we might exhibit behaviors that you understandably take personally.

When you think about your man and try to analyze his thought process, you need to understand that sometimes there is not a lot going on up there. Yes, there are some deep, thinking men out there who consider all the ramifications of their actions, but most men are not that complicated in their thinking. In fact, if you see your man stare out the window or off into the distance during a song that you both used to love, don't think that he is bored with you or that your relationship is on a downward spiral. He might just be zoning out or preoccupied with his own struggles.

Keep in mind that no matter how it seems, it is very unlikely that what we are doing is purposely trying to hurt you. You might think that men have this inbuilt insensitivity and a need to cause you distress, but that is not the case at all. We are not trying to hurt you when we do the things that we do. We do the things we do with little regard for what will happen to those around us. That's because we are so focused on the action that we do not add other people into the equation. Of course, that is not a valid excuse for neglectful behavior, but it is something you might want to take into account.

RULE TWENTY FOUR

Confidence Can Be A Smokescreen

For us guys, sometimes our confidence is not what it seems. There is every reason for someone to fake confidence, especially around the opposite sex. This is a concept that we have already touched on in this book, but you have to understand that guys need to be confident in order to attract the woman they want. Both parties need to have confidence in themselves and believe that they are good enough for the other person, or else the chase will be one-sided and quite short.

But you should also understand that we are not always as confident as we appear. Men and women are pretty different in terms of how they look at the world and how they experience emotional events. Both genders experience self-esteem issues even far into adulthood. Most of the time, the men you will be dating will have overcome their adolescent shortcomings and will be confident in many aspects of their life. However, there will be times that you come across an area where a man may not be very confident at all.

The thing that you need to know about this is that we tend to act overconfident when we are not feeling very confident. Using this tactic, we are hoping that our false confidence will disguise what we are really feeling inside. We are hoping that by overcompensating, we are able to hide our deficiencies. So you are going to notice a difference in our behavior on some occasions. You might well view that overconfidence as cockiness. You may feel that your man is acting like a jerk when in fact you might have just breached a sensitive area and made him feel self-conscious, hence triggering a need to overcompensate.

Men get self-conscious about their self-image just as women do. While women tend to be more open about it and take steps to solve it, men also think about how members of the opposite sex — or the same sex in the case of non-heterosexual relationships — perceive them. He may think deeply about off-hand comments that you made in regards to his looks. You may have said something completely innocent that he internalized the wrong way. For example, if he has long hair and you tell him that you think he would look extra sexy with a trim, this may be perceived as an insult towards his look rather than a compliment of how well he presents himself overall.

When this happens, men can act defensive, arrogant and often even overbearing. They can even sometimes act like jerks and try to drive you away because they feel hurt. You need to understand that your man has this sensitivity, and look out for warning signs that he is feeling self-conscious or out of his comfort zone. This field is littered with mines, and there is no way to avoid them completely, but the best thing that you can do is simply reassure him that you love him for how he is now, without feeling he needs to drastically change anything.

RULE TWENTY FIVE

We Want Respect

Respect is a huge concept in a man's life. If you want to take the most extreme example possible, think about the prison movies or TV shows that you have seen. Respect is the currency of trade in those prisons. When a man has the respect of others, he feels powerful and self-confident and is ready to take on the world.

Of course, the real world is not a prison. The illustration of prison is used because the concept is more exaggerated in jail so that you can see it more clearly. In the real world, you are not respected by other people for stabbing someone who may have ratted you out to the police! Instead, you may be respected for hiring a prospective employee from under the nose of a competitor, or for your income, or for your choice of spouse or even for your charity work.

The relationship perspective is completely different for women and men. Women want to be cherished. They want their men to protect them and to consider them above any other woman. On the other hand, men want to be respected. With men that have abusive tendencies, this is often where that abuse starts — from a perceived lack of respect. If a man has convinced himself that his significant other is disrespecting him, he may respond in a multitude of negative ways. Of course, physical violence should never be an option, and most men will not consider it, but he may make comments, offer insults, close himself off or simply ignore you —   particularly if the relationship is fairly new.

We touched on being grateful in an earlier chapter, but you may not have realized at the time just how much men are looking for appreciation, validation and respect. They need to know that you think highly of them and that they are worthy of your respect. Women that belittle their men are going to find themselves without a partner in the long run, as respect is a fundamental factor in a man's hierarchy of needs.

So make sure that you keep this concept in mind. Women want to be cherished and men want to be respected. These are two completely different concepts because they come from two completely different mindsets. A man thrives emotionally when he feels he is being respected, and is prone to insecurity and negativity when this key factor is absent. Of course, you should never respect someone who doesn't deserve it just to preserve a relationship. In cases such as these, where mutual respect is absent, the relationship is built on sand and it's just a matter of time before it crumbles.

RULE TWENTY SIX

Don't Push So Hard To Change Us

Change is a funny thing. You have probably already encountered women who say they have met a man but he needs to be "trained". This could be considered offensive, but women still believe that they can change the men they are with. This is sometimes the reason why women find themselves in abusive relationships. They may initially see the warning signs of a man who will become abusive later, but they believe that their love is so strong that they can exercise their will over the guy and get him to change his ways.

In other words, women often fall for the broken or slightly damaged man with the notion that they can be rescued. This is a common romantic trope that is a basic plot for countless books and films. The broken man may have been hurt in the past. He may have sworn off relationships completely and is not willing to pursue them any longer. But the woman who goes after him believes that she can change all that. She believes that she alone has the power to heal his heart and make him believe in love once again. While this is the central plot of many of the romance novels that you can find on the shelves of your local bookstore, it isn't reality.

Here is what you need to understand. First, we know when you are trying to change us. We are completely aware of the strategies you use to try to manipulate us into acting a certain way. Now, there are, of course, certain things that we are willing to change. These are small things, though. These are not huge parts of our character or persona that define us as individuals. A man may adapt his behavior in a relationship, such as being more considerate and courteous. He may even be willing to move to another city or take on a second job in order to accumulate the resources required to move forward with the relationship.

But when you start trying to alter the fundamental character and personality of a man, you are going to run into problems. We realize that we need to adapt and compromise in a relationship, but if you try to get us to give up huge parts of our identity such as watching sports and hanging out with the guys regularly, you are going to find yourself disappointed. We are going to resist when you try to mold us into something that we are simply not and can never be. From the outset you should largely accept us for who we are, with all of our faults and quirks, and have the understanding that you may only be able to change a limited number of peripheral things.

This goes both ways. Just as we would never want you to try to change us into someone that watches romantic weepies instead of the big football game, we would never ask you to give up your interests or hanging out with your friends. We would never ask you to give up your main hobbies. If you find a good man, he is going to be accepting of who you are and, although he may encourage you to change certain things, he is not going to try to force it on you. He is also not going to try to change the core of who you are to conform to his desires. This is not a sign of a healthy relationship.

PART FIVE

Secrets Of The Bedroom

Being intimate is one of the biggest parts of a relationship. When it comes to forging closeness and intimacy, how you act in the bedroom is going to count for a lot. There are some details you need to understand about what goes on in the bedroom that could help your relationship flourish. For example, you might think that performance issues are restricted to a very small portion of the population, but the truth is that nearly every man experiences these issues at some point or another, and it usually has nothing at all to do with you. That's just one example of the topics that we will be covering in this section.

Getting a relationship into the bedroom is a milestone for every man. However, if you allow this too soon, he could get bored and leave as the thrill and chase elements have evaporated. If you wait until the appropriate time, he is going to be invested in the relationship mentally and emotionally, which will makes things far more special. Only you can decide when the appropriate time is, but the odds are good that if you play it out as long as possible — such as at least five or six dates — then the chances of your relationship lasting are much higher.

You can do a lot of things outside of the bedroom that don't involve sex, and you can draw out the act of intimacy for as long as you think is sensible, as long as you do not lead the guy on. Let him know right up front that you will have sex with him when you're ready, and not before. That way, the ball is completely in your court and, hopefully, you will not be subject to undue pressure. He may still try to convince you to have sex, but as long as you stick to your stated plan that you will make the decision when you are ready, there will be no hostility and he will still pursue you with interest.

As mentioned, in the meantime, you can do a whole lot of different things that will maintain the spice in your relationship. Men talk about a base system. First base is usually making out, second base is touching under the clothes, third base is usually stimulation of the intimate areas, while fourth base, also known as home base, is considered full sex.

One thing to keep in mind as you read through this section is that there are certain behaviors while getting to know each other physically that can have a major impact on the relationship. For example, how you respond to performance issues or your general attitude towards sex can significantly change the dynamic of your relationship. This section will give you tips that will help you avoid the rough patches. Let's begin.

RULE TWENTY SEVEN

Men Don't Consider
Porn A Big Deal

The use of porn is a big deal in some relationships and we definitely need to address it here. The simple fact is that pornography is not that big of a deal for guys, but it is often a very big deal for the women who have to contend with it. That's because men and women generally look at pornography from two widely different perspectives. We will take a look at each of those perspectives to show the differences and examine where couples may find some common ground.

But first we have to discuss pornography addiction. The occasional use of pornography is not the same thing as addiction. Men can use pornography to enhance lovemaking and sexual arousal or to aid in masturbation. Porn addiction means that you cannot orgasm without viewing it or thinking about it. If the man you are in a relationship with has a pornography addiction, then you are going to struggle in your relationship. You definitely have a right to be concerned if this is the case.

However, if we are talking about the casual use of pornography, you should understand how men think about it. For a man, pornography is simply erotic entertainment. There is nothing personal about it. There are no elements of it that we feel detracts from any healthy relationships we are in. We can separate pornography from our relationship because it doesn't mean much more beyond fantasy escapism. It is simply a tool that we use to get aroused and usually masturbate with. There is no emotional relationship with pornography. There is no love or a danger of falling in love with any of the participants we view on screen.

Pornography can be interpreted as something quite different to a woman. When her partner views porn, she can take it as a personal insult. She feels that he is choosing a porn star over her and favoring a glamorized body ideal over a natural female form which has not been enhanced. She can view it as a threat to her relationship, as she would never be able to compete with the fantasy images on screen. To her, it's a form of cheating and a betrayal of the implicit oath to be respectful and faithful once in a relationship.

What you have to do is find a way to work around the viewing of pornography. If it's a deal-breaker for you, then that's how it is. If it's something that you simply cannot accept, then you may have to give him an ultimatum or walk away. However, if you put your foot down and tell your significant other that he is not allowed to view pornography, that stance comes with dangers. This is not because you are potentially taking away the pornography itself, but because you are not giving your man a choice. When you give your man an ultimatum, he feels as if his agency and self-determination as a man has been removed. To the male mind, this can be construed as you not trusting or respecting him enough to allow him to make the choice.

The best way to handle this thorny subject is simply by talking very openly about it and letting your partner know, in no uncertain terms, exactly how you feel. If the two of you can talk it out, and he can explain how he regards pornography, and you can explain to him your perspective, then there is a good chance that you can work out some sort of compromise. There is also the possibility that he may agree to give it up altogether in order to make you happy. In either case, you will be giving him the choice and he will appreciate you for that.

RULE TWENTY EIGHT

Take Charge In The Bedroom

Men are fairly simple creatures in some regards, but when it comes to the bedroom, things can get complicated. Because historically guys have been viewed as the take-charge gender in heterosexual relationships, women can still expect them to take exclusive charge in the bedroom. While some men are perfectly happy to fulfill this role and even prefer it, there are others who would prefer things to be the other way around, occasionally or all the time. In addition, men want you to be happy in the bedroom. It might not always seem that way, but in our heart of hearts, we want you to get as much pleasure from lovemaking as possible, and that means sometimes you taking the lead and showing us what you prefer.

There is a good analogy in the television series *Game of Thrones*. The great Dothraki leader Khal Drogo married his Khaleesi (wife) Daenerys, and at the end of the night he took what he wanted from her. He bent her over the bed and did his business without any regard for her as a lover or even as a human being. Over the next weeks, she spent her days learning enough of his language so that eventually when he came in to perform his business, she stood up to him and told him that they would be face-to-face, and that tonight, she wanted him to look at her. If you watch the show after that, you will notice that their relationship changes drastically, and that was the moment when they actually began falling in love.

This is a clear, if slightly dramatic, example of how you can take charge in the bedroom in order to spark more romance and ensure that your physical and emotional needs are met. Your partner should know what you want in the bedroom. You need to tell him — or better yet, show him — exactly what you would like. In this respect, women tend to give hints rather than straight explanations and men do not always register these hints or respond to them. Sex is a loaded subject and we all come to it with our own level of reservation and frankness, so discussing it is not always the easiest of endeavors. But, trust me, he will be thankful if you give him directions in the bedroom and he'll be glad to accommodate them if he cares for you.

In addition to making him feel like a considerate lover, giving him the information necessary to make you happy is going to work in both of your favors. When he is able to turn you on, it enhances his sexual experience as well. In other words, we get off knowing that the other person is getting off. In fact, for many men, there is nothing sexier than a woman who is completely turned on by what they are able to do.

Even if your man is a bit of a control freak in the bedroom, try taking charge once or twice. He might find that he actually enjoys the loss of control that he experiences, especially if he is in control of many other aspects of his life. Many men are surprised to find that they actually enjoy being the subservient one under the sheets, and women may find confidence and sexual fulfillment in being in charge. The key is to be open and experiment until you find what works for the both of you.

RULE TWENTY NINE

Don't Panic If We Can't Finish

Two issues that can occur in the bedroom that no man really wants to talk about is erectile dysfunction and the inability to orgasm. The problem is that, because society does not openly discuss these issues, women believe that when a man is unable to achieve an erection or reach orgasm that there might be something amiss in the relationship or there could be a medical concern. Women can also be forgiven for thinking that their partner no longer desires them to the same extent as before. But, in truth, that is rarely the case.

There are going to be times when we simply cannot finish (or start) in the bedroom. This often happens when we are under a great deal of stress. If your mind is on other things and, at the same time, you feel under pressure to perform, then you are going to have a very difficult time concentrating and getting your body to respond how you would wish. Imagination, thoughts and arousal go hand in hand. Men that are contemplating worrying and repetitive thoughts — as we all do from time to time — while attempting to perform any physical act are either going to take a long time to get there or they are not going to perform with the same level of potency as usual.

Stress is not the only factor that can influence whether your man is able to perform. Tiredness can be a huge factor. If your man feels exhausted, he is not going to be able to perform in the bedroom. Unfortunately, due to the high cost of living in western societies, many people work long hours and sometimes sleep is a luxury. The key takeaway is not to take it personally and view the current difficulty as a fault with either your partner or yourself. As a man, there's every chance he will be mortified when he realizes that his body is unable to do what is required during intimacy.

So, how do you deal with a situation where your man cannot perform?

First, make sure that he knows it is no big deal in your eyes. You can even be the one to reassure him that it happens to every guy at some point or another, because of stress or other unavoidable life situations. If he is not aware of this, he may look up the research later on his own and feel better about himself. However, your man is probably going to be embarrassed about the situation in the moment.

But if you continue to hold him, this will let him know that you are not overly concerned about it and, more importantly, that you love him no matter what his body will or will not do at that particular moment. Don't feel sorry for him or get angry. Definitely do not ridicule him. Just make sure he knows that you still desire and want him and that you are perfectly happy with cuddling or other forms of closeness for the time being.

PART SIX

Dos & Don'ts

In any relationship, there are things that you learn to do and learn not to do. The things that you learn to do are behaviors that will help you have a smoother relationship, and the things that you learn to avoid are disruptions that will throw up roadblocks on your path to happiness. That is exactly what we will be covering in the next section.

There are definitely things you should do to indicate that you are the woman that your guy should keep. When you do these actions, he sees you as someone who he could actually spend his life with and potentially marry, because he feels that you understand him. Every person — both male and female — longs to be understood and appreciated for who they are. When you follow some of the suggestions that are laid out in this section, you will be showing him that you deeply understand him and are compatible with him.

This section is also filled with actions and behaviors you should avoid. To be totally honest, there are certain things that women do that drive men to distraction. These are often deal-breakers — behaviors that make us not want a relationship on any level with the woman who exhibits them. These are actions that raise such big red flags that we have no desire to be with the person no matter how attractive they are.

Women often do not even realize that they are acting in these ways. In some cases, they even think that they are helping the relationship by indulging in this behavior. Well, it's time for some honest and brutal truth. Here we go.

RULE THIRTY

Don't Be Obsessive

A behavior that some women exhibit that men probably dislike more than almost any other is obsessiveness. This habit is often related to some of the self-esteem issues that we have touched on in this book. If you show obsessiveness it can make men think of you as insecure at best. At worst, it could raise flags over your emotional and psychological stability. For men, obsessiveness is not only a turnoff in a relationship, it can be downright scary and an indication of potential drama to come down the road.

You need to understand that there is a major difference between healthy jealousy and obsessiveness. We understand healthy jealousy. We feel jealous too. If we check out a pretty woman who is walking by, which is something that guys often do and find difficult to control, we understand that you will get annoyed. It is perfectly reasonable for you to get angry in that instance. It is also reasonable for you to feel jealous about our exes or be concerned if we are socializing with a woman who isn't you — even if it is for work.

But healthy jealousy should not be allowed to grow into obsessiveness. If you see that your boyfriend is checking out other women or socializing with someone from work who happens to be female, this does not automatically give you license to begin looking through his cell phone, stalking him on social media and checking on him whenever he goes out. If you suspect infidelity, then this is another matter altogether. However, if you have no reason to mistrust your partner, nothing good will come from exhibiting obsessiveness. It is a behavior we detest and triggers massive warning signs for us. If you want to be jealous, that is your right, and it is often a justified natural reaction, but check yourself when it comes to acting on your feelings.

Also, sometimes obsessiveness doesn't have to center around jealousy. You can be obsessive without being jealous. If you track your man for no reason at all other than you want to know his every move, or you are constantly trying to get him to tell you how he feels or what he is thinking, to a guy this also falls under the banner of obsessiveness. I'm not saying this assessment is correct, and people have different definitions as to what constitutes obsessiveness. However, while we can appreciate that you care about us, we don't want to be the center of your universe and the only thing that you focus on. This is an uncomfortable position for anyone.

So, when you find yourself becoming overly jealous, intrusive or bordering on the obsessive, take a step back and realize that, unless you suspect infidelity, people are innocent until proven guilty. When it comes to actual cheating, you will find out eventually if he is being dishonest with you, and then you can end the relationship. But if you pursue obsessive behavior when there is no cause, you may end up destroying a potentially great relationship.

RULE THIRTY ONE

Don't Say "I Love You" Every Five Seconds

Women sometimes say "I love you" way too much. This phrase has a great deal of power behind it. It is a potent statement that carries a great deal of emotion and meaning. When you use it too much, it loses its power. It is like a magic incantation that diminishes if you use it for everything. Guys often get frustrated when a woman says this phrase to them too often, especially when the goal of saying it is to get their man to say it back to them.

Now, of course, I'm not saying that you should never use the phrase "I love you". In fact, you should certainly use it in a meaningful relationship, but you have to be smart about it. That means learning when and where the right time to say it is. In addition, your actions need to match your words. Actions speak way louder than spoken platitudes, and you should be able to demonstrate your love with your actions in a much clearer and powerful way than simply using the phrase verbally.

When to say it for the first time is a tricky

subject. Some people say that you will know when you are in love, but others have had difficulty with this. Only you will be able to figure out if you are at a point in your relationship where you should say this key phrase. You definitely want to make sure that your partner is on the same page as you before you say it. Also, don't use it when you mean something else like "I really like you" or "My hormones are raging right now and I feel like I'm on cloud nine because of you". You want it to mean that you have actually fallen in love with the person.

There are a few pointers that you can follow in order to make sure that you are not saying "I love you" too much. First of all, avoid saying it right after having sex. There is a huge emotional surge that happens after sex, especially in women, and it is easy to think that you might be in love because you've had a good lovemaking session and hormones are firing. However, the two are not the same.

Don't say it when you have had too much to drink or when you are on medication. It's not very romantic and you may not even remember it the next day. When you do say it, keep it simple rather than making it some grand gesture that you copy from a romantic comedy. You don't have to shout from the rooftops that you love a guy, and if he does not reciprocate it's going to be pretty embarrassing for you! Finally, don't over think it. In fact, don't think about it at all, just let it come naturally. When the time is right, you will be able to feel that this is the moment. It will be natural and truly special.

RULE THIRTY TWO

Don't Resent Our Achievements

There are individuals out there who feel resentful when their significant other achieves their goals. For example, a young couple is living in an apartment on a shoestring budget, but they are still very happy. But suddenly the guy starts getting promotions at work and begins making more money than his partner. Rather than celebrating his success, the woman becomes insecure and resentful. I can tell you that for men, it is extremely frustrating and confusing to be with a woman who is resentful of their progress. We simply don't understand the logic behind this attitude, and we would much rather be with someone who is supportive of our achievements.

Now, I am well aware that guys can suffer from the exact same problem and be just as mean-spirited and insecure. However, this is a book intended for women, so I'm approaching it from that perspective.

Even though your behavior might be a mystery to us guys, psychologists have some insight into it. The theory goes like this: when you first meet someone, it can often seem like you have similar drives and desires on the surface. But once you start dating, you might find that your goals and drives are not as similar as you thought they were. Moreover, you might realize that you are not as committed to your goals as he is to his. In other words, he has a lot more desire for success in certain areas of his life, while you are just hoping to achieve some of the things that you want.

There is nothing fundamentally wrong with this, except that it can breed resentment when he starts achieving his goals because his desire was so much stronger. What his success is basically doing is feeding your insecurities. Every time he achieves something, your mind takes it as a personal insult and shows you the things that you have not been able to accomplish in comparison with his achievements.

Unfortunately, this dynamic isn't rare and is particularly prevalent among men. As women have become more accepted in the workplace and have reached positions of power such as CEO or upper management, men have had to adjust their gender expectations. Many men are still threatened by the success of a woman. This is often fueled by the archaic view that women are somehow inferior and should not be able to achieve the same level of success as them.

Luckily, this backwards view is not the case for women. When women become jealous or resentful it is more likely because the success of their man can highlight their own insecurities and make them realize that they are playing catch-up. But no matter what the reasoning behind it, it is important that you support us in our accomplishments and that you do not become offended by them. Any relationship where one partner resents the positive things happening in the other's life is doomed to fail.

RULE THIRTY THREE

Don't Do Emotional Cheating

Emotional cheating is definitely something that you want to avoid in a relationship. It basically means doing things purposely that would cause the other person to become jealous. You may not technically be doing anything wrong, but you are acting in a way that provokes a reaction. For us guys, this hurts us a lot.

When we get into a relationship, we know the reality is that now we must stop hanging out with other women. We cannot spend hours in the company of another lady, even if she is just a friend. We cannot be inviting them over to our house when we are the only one there and we cannot go out to activities with other women alone. We know that this would hurt you and make you jealous. Even if it is completely innocent, it is still going to put a strain on the relationship. When we start dating someone, we accept this as part of the unspoken contract.

But the same goes for women as well. We are going to get jealous if you go out with other guys, in whatever context. If you spend time with other men, do activities with them and are in their presence for hours at a time, it is going to make us jealous and hurt. Even if there is absolutely nothing inappropriate going on, it is still a form of emotional cheating in our eyes.

What's more, it is unlikely that we are going to talk about the problem we have with you going out with guy friends. We think it sounds petty and we fear we would simply come across as jealous and controlling. So, potentially, you will be able to go out over and over again and we will just stay silent and brood about it. But inside there is turmoil.

Emotional cheating might be taking place simply because you are not considering your partner enough when you choose your social activities, where you go or what you do once you get there. Emotional cheating might be going out with friends and getting extremely drunk, leaving us to wonder what might have been going on while you were away from us and in that state.

Emotional cheating might also be when you hang out with friends who we know don't like us very much. We are left to silently ponder what might be being said about us behind our back. There are many ways that emotional cheating can happen, but just be aware that it hurts us every time.

RULE THIRTY FOUR

Do Shut Up Sometimes

The comedian Chris Rock famously claimed that men need only three things: food, sex and silence.

While these words were said in jest, like all humor, there's an underlying truth here.

Men *need* silence in their life from time to time. It's a much-needed opportunity for us to wind down mentally and recharge our emotional batteries. It also gives us the space to process our thoughts and feelings, and deal with any pressing issues that are preoccupying our minds.

But, hey, we get it. Women like to talk and share their feelings, and open communication is the basis for a solid relationship. However, the point is that incessant jabbering all the time is not the way to strengthen a bond. To us, it's a form of inescapable torture that brings down the quality of our life. To be sure, there are times when we like to talk just as much as you, and really get out all we have brewing inside of us. But there also needs to be peace and quiet.

You have to include silent spaces into your

relationship where the guy gets a chance to withdraw into his own world for a while. When he's had a mental rest and been allowed to reset his bearings, you'll find he's once more the caring and engaging guy you were no doubt first attracted to.

When we don't get this space, you are going to get an irritated grouch on your hands that will be short-tempered and snappy. This is because we feel as though we are being constantly bombarded and our partner, who is meant to be the closest to us, just doesn't understand who we are and what we need in the moment.

I can tell you from firsthand experience that constantly being subjected to a flood of communication when we are not in the right state to handle it will have us looking for an escape route. This could mean going to the bar, a sports event or video gaming with a friend. While none of these options are necessarily bad in and of themselves, the fact that we are using them to escape an unhappy domestic situation is a grim portent. You certainly don't want this avoidance behavior to become a habit.

As I have made clear earlier in this book, silence and personal space does not mean there is anything wrong with your relationship. It isn't a sign that either party has lost interest or that your relationship is dying — in fact, the truth is quite the opposite. Allowing for quiet periods is a sign of empathy, maturity and trust between two people. It means you know each other well enough to read when your partner needs some space, and you are selfless enough to give them this time, even if your natural impulse is to engage with them.

This goes back to men and women being wired differently. Relationships suffer when there's a fundamental misunderstanding that gender differences are hard-coded through evolution. Even though the very notion of gender is changing at a dramatic pace in modern society, there's no escaping that men and women have vastly differing mindsets. You need to use this to your advantage in demonstrating empathy and understanding, otherwise you are going to run into trouble.

Having the mistaken view that because you feel a certain way, that must be how everyone else functions, is a recipe for broken relationships — whether that be with a spouse, friend or family member. Sometimes you need to be the bigger person and put your needs on the back burner in order for someone else to get what they need. This gesture is unlikely to go unnoticed or unappreciated by the other person, and you can expect similar kind gestures and selfless acts from them going forward. This give-and-take is the basis for a rock-solid union.

Remember, for your relationship, sometimes silence really is golden.

RULE THIRTY FIVE

Don't Reveal Our Secrets

I don't think it's an outrageous statement to say that women like to talk. Gossip even!

It's also true that women are far more open in their private conversations than men tend to be. It's in female nature to share and discuss feelings and events in order to find a resolution to a problem, or simply for the cathartic act of sharing. This open dialogue builds trust, closeness and community among social groups and has been a feature of societies for millennia.

While sharing is an important social dynamic, there's a line that you must never cross when it comes to your relationship. Namely, sharing the secrets of your partner. This constitutes the ultimate betrayal.

It can be difficult for many men to open up about their feelings, or any matters that are intensely personal to them. Society very much still portrays men as the strong and stable ones, who are expected to succeed in the world and provide for their family. It can take a great deal of time and trust for us to divulge information about our families, health or any other personally important matters. We often fear being judged, ridiculed or not being able to live up to the image of the strong man who can take on the world.

So to divulge a secret, to even our partner, is not something that we do lightly. If that trust is then betrayed, we consider it the ultimate kick in the teeth and our faith in the other person is badly shaken — if not destroyed. We can say we forgive our partner but, in truth, the damage is done and the relationship can never go back to where it was before the betrayal.

Your significant other will be unlikely to ever trust you again with information that is important to him. Once two people can't share their innermost thoughts and feelings in a relationship, then it is doomed, because that is the very definition of what a relationship should be. The relationship may limp along for a while longer but, in the mind of the man, he is always wary of the next betrayal and on his guard to watch what he says — in case it is broadcast to a wider audience.

So if you learn that his sister is getting a divorce, that he failed to win a promotion at work or that he occasionally suffers from depressive episodes, that information is sacrosanct. It's not to be shared or turned into a topic for discussion —

even if you are genuinely trying to help your partner by looking for solutions from other people. This is not a valid excuse.

Once he learns that his confidence was betrayed — and it is very likely this will happen as people naturally want to talk about "juicy" gossip — there is no going back and making it right again. A landmine has just gone off in your relationship and it is very likely that the damage to his trust will be so severe that it cannot be mended.

As already mentioned, swearing your friends to secrecy and asking them not to disclose what you have shared is a fool's errand. At this point you have no control over how the information will be used or spread. What if you have a falling out with a friend who knows your partner's secrets? What do you think the likely outcome is going to be? Now you have to live in fear in case your decision ever comes back to bite you. Do you want to anticipate a bomb going off in your relationship at any moment? What kind of life is that?

So while they say "sharing is caring", sharing your partner's secrets is the ultimate way to show that you don't actually care — about his feelings, his trust, his personal life and ultimately about your relationship together. Never do it.

RULE THIRTY SIX

Don't Pressure Us To Get Married

Men can be self-centered creatures when it comes to the priorities in their life. Their primary drive is often to make the most of themselves. In the psychology books this is referred to as "self-actualization", which is defined as "the realization or fulfillment of one's talents and potentialities".

So how does this relate to the marriage question?

Well, marriage, kids and a settled life are often the furthest thing from a guy's mind when he is chasing his own aspirations. In fact, when it comes to personal or career development, having a wife or young children can be viewed as a hindrance on his path.

That's not to say that settling down is not on his horizon at all. But you have to understand that until he feel he has achieved certain goals he has set for himself, he will not be receptive to talk of marriage. In fact, I know from many of my friends that pressure to get engaged when the man is just not ready is a recipe for bitterness, resentment and unhappiness in the relationship.

So this is often a question of timing. If you feel you need to tie the knot in the near future or there's the understandable biological imperative on your part, trying to lock down commitment from a guy on the beginning of his self-actualization journey is simply not going to work.

In this case, you have to select a potential partner who has the mental space and willingness to accommodate a life partner and who is no longer focused solely on his personal goals. In fact, you could say that his personal goals have now shifted to becoming a good husband, father and provider.

Yes, you might able to strong-arm or guilt trip your partner into marrying you, but that's a formula for an unsuccessful union. He was never ready to take this leap in the first place and he did not complete his self-actualization journey. Now, within the confines of the marriage, he will feel restricted, burdened and might take the view that he was forced onto a life path that he was not ready to travel. Not at this stage of his life, at any rate.

Certain cultures and religious groups put a lot of pressure on young women to tie the knot as soon as possible. They view relationships outside the umbrella of marriage as somehow immoral. This puts a lot of pressure on women to marry quickly, which in turn ends up becoming a point of contention in the relationship. As I have mentioned before, there's little to be gained in the long-term by forcing marriage on someone who is not prepared for its restrictions and responsibilities.

Often, men find the prospect of marriage downright scary — even if they are at the stage of life where they are open to settling down. Rampant divorce rates, the prospect of possibly losing half your wealth and the cost of raising children are just some of the factors that can shake resolve. In fact, there's a growing movement among some men know as MGTOW — or "Men Going Their Own Way". This philosophy swears off marriage and long-term relationships altogether due to the potential downsides for men!

So you need to understand that, for men, marriage can be a touchy and loaded subject. You need to broach the topic with tact and sensitivity. Aggressiveness or ultimatums will likely scare your partner off. Men generally want to settle down when they are ready, but they often need to be eased into the prospect. Softly, softly is the way to achieve best results.

RULE THIRTY SEVEN

Don't Try To Be
"One Of The Guys"

It's understandable that you want to be part of your significant other's life. You may want to participate in his interests, get to know his family or try to have a greater appreciation of his working day. That's all for the good and helps to build a stronger bond.

However, trying to be a part of his circle of friends is entering dangerous territory. Let's not go too far here. This does not mean you must have no contact with his friends or acquaintances, or you should be cold and dismissive towards them. You need to get along with his friends as they are likely to be a permanent part of his life. There will also be social occasions when you are all together as a group, so good relations are important.

However, don't try to be one of the guys. This is for two key reasons.

The first is that your partner needs time away from you to connect with his friends and be immersed in male energy. This is his time to recharge and also seek advice and insight into his relationship from his peers. If you are there all the time, this cannot happen. He effectively has no break from you and no opportunity to decompress from the responsibilities of being in a relationship.

Human beings have many different facets to their personality depending on the social group they find themselves in. Your partner cannot be his authentic self with his friends if you are there to potentially judge him for his behavior. He will find this scrutiny restricting and come to resent your presence, even while you feel you are being a good partner by getting to know his friends. This is *his* time and you need to respect that.

The second reason is that being a partner and being a friend are two different roles. His friends may be loud, noisy, sport types, in whose company your partner lets off steam. If you then try to fit in with this dynamic by becoming louder, brasher or trying to keep pace when it comes to the consumption of alcohol, then are you really expressing your true nature? What's more, his perception of you is going to shift radically if you start behaving in ways that he hasn't seen before. It's likely that the qualities and experiences he is looking for with friends is not the same things he is looking for in a partner.

If you suddenly go from being a demure and ladylike partner to a sweary, beer-swilling "pal", then that's a big psychological adjustment to make. It also smacks more than slightly of desperation and trying too hard.

Your partner needs a life away from you. Allowing him this time and space is essential for a healthy relationship. If you begin to crowd into this area — even though your intentions may be noble — there could be a string of negative consequences. Stay away.

RULE THIRTY EIGHT

Do Say What's On Your Mind

I don't think it's sexist to say that men are not the most empathetic gender. Subtlety and suggestion don't really work with us — we are simply terrible at reading the cues and hints. If you need to say something to us, you need to come right out and say it. If there's something on your mind and bothering you about the relationship, we really want to hear about it. We would much rather be in the loop than in the dark. It's in our nature.

If you keep your feelings bottled up inside, sure, you may avoid a disagreement or argument in the moment. But what you are actually doing is creating a pattern of behavior that will become very hard to break. Suffocating your feelings will only build up your internal resentment until you reach a point where it has to all come flooding out in a sudden torrent.

Men — who, remember, are not very good at reading the signs — will be blindsided by this sudden outpouring of anger and frustrating. To us, it will be frightening, bewildering and could cause us to question whether we really knew the person who was meant to be the closest to us. Don't let it get to this stage.

Men tend to be very practical in their thinking, and confronting an issue in its early stages makes perfect sense to us. Imagine you bought a new house but discovered a tiny crack in the brickwork. Over the weeks you notice this crack becoming bigger and bigger until it threatens to eventually bring the entire wall down. At the outset, would you just let the crack go on growing, knowing that the problem will only get worse and worse? Or would you take action to deal with the issue while it is still small and manageable?

In the same way, don't threaten the stability of your relationship by allowing small issues to fester until you can't take any more and something dramatic has to happen. It's more than likely that your partner is completely oblivious to your specific concern and has no idea that it is bothering you so much. If it is something about his behavior that is causing you concern, then he has no incentive to change his ways if he has no idea how you are feeling — or even what the issue is!

When it comes to relationships, men, who can be inherently self-focused, sometimes need a bit of direction and guidance to ensure things run smoothly for both partners. It's not something we take offense to when we're given the odd pointer now and then. In fact, we welcome the hints, as we know reading the opposite sex is not our strong point.

When you speak your mind it also shows us that you take the relationship seriously and that you want to resolve any issues that could potentially present an obstacle to a shared future. It also conveys bravery, honesty and openness — all great qualities that any person would love to have in a partner. Conversely, keeping your views hidden could be seen as demonstrating dishonesty, secrecy and weakness, which I'm sure you would agree would be a turnoff for anyone seeking a lasting relationship. So sometimes caring means rocking the boat and getting your feelings off your chest.

I'm sure if your partner was unhappy about some aspect of your relationship, you would want to know. You might not necessarily agree with his assessment, but you would be happier addressing the issue than being with someone who is harboring a hidden resentment. Well, we feel the exact same way. We prefer honesty, even if it's about something that makes us uncomfortable. Get it out into the open.

RULE THIRTY NINE

Don't Hit Us — Ever

You might think it's only playful, you might do it in jest, or you might think we are big and tough enough to take it. But the truth is that you should never hit your partner.

No, we don't think it's funny. No, we don't think it's cute. No, we don't think it's playful. Hitting us stirs up the same feelings as you would experience if we hit you. It's an act of aggression and a violation of what should be a supportive and caring relationship.

Guys like to live up to the stereotype of being strong and resilient. If you hit us, we might seem to take it in our stride, and even act as if it's all playful and light. However, after you have laid your hands on us with the intention to inflict pain, the relationship will never be the same again.

At this point you will be viewed as a person who is both willing and able to hit us. There is a boundary that you have crossed which marks you as someone who we are not entirely safe and secure around. The fact that you have hit us once puts us on our guard that it may happen again in future. If you lash out in the heat of an argument, then that says a lot about how you deal with conflict and your ability to resolve issues in a peaceful manner.

Violence — whether it's bullying in the playground or physical discipline from a strict parent — leaves an indelible mark on a person. Both men and women associate the act of being struck with dark and unpleasant times in their life, when they were victimized or made to feel helpless.

What emotions do you think are going to surface when you hit a guy — even in a playful manner? The act will automatically activate negative memories and feelings. Perhaps feelings of inadequacy when your partner was younger and felt scared, intimidated or was unable to fight back.

Physical sensations are powerful triggers that bring up the same feelings as when we experienced those same sensations in the past. And hitting is going to bring up (even if it's subconsciously) very unpleasant emotions. This is a sure-fire way to sabotage your relationship.

The act of hitting also conveys a fundamental lack of respect for the other person. We have been conditioned through the education system to view hitting as wrong and a form of bullying. If it has no place in wider society, it should have no place in a relationship. In fact, a relationship should be a refuge from harm — not the cause of it.

It might not be fashionable to say this in the current climate, but hitting a guy can be an effective way to emasculate him. Men still like to be seen as the physically stronger gender, which can provide and protect. That sense of self is threatened if a man is physically attacked by a woman. Now, I'm not saying that it is your role to be meek, submissive or accept out-of-date gender roles. However, I would ask you to think twice before hitting in any manner. There might be no going back from the psychological impact it will have on your partner.

There is a fine line. I'm not saying never be playful or physical, and a lot depends on the personality and upbringing of your partner. Some people are naturally less sensitive than others. But as a general rule, always take a cautious approach until you have established the types of physical contact that are not seen as threatening or aggressive. Then try to stay within these boundaries.

RULE FORTY

Don't Only Remember The One Thing We Did Wrong

Sometimes a guy just can't win. The romantic playbook tells us there's a list of things we have to pay attention to — compliment her appearance, buy her flowers regularly, do the driving, carry the shopping, cook once in a while. So, if in the midst of trying to juggle all these tasks, your guy doesn't get it right on one thing, is it fair to chew him out?

People become complacent in relationships, so all the little things he does to make your life easier and a little more pleasant get taken for granted. Then, if he leaves the dishes in the sink one day or forgets to mail that package you need to return, you feel he had one simple task to do — and he couldn't even manage that! You become blind to all the other duties he attends to make the relationship run smoothly. You lose sight of the bigger picture.

This is not to say that you are acting viciously or being mean for the sake of being mean. The fact is that it is human nature to become accustomed to things that people do for us regularly. It becomes a background part of our lives, which we don't give much thought to.

So when on occasion he does not live up to your expectations, ask yourself, is this really such a big deal? Look at the larger picture and take account of the things he does for you and has done for you in the past. Is this one thing worth starting an argument over in that bigger context?

Also, to make mistakes and forget things once in a while is human. No one can be expected to get it right 100 percent of the time. Have you never made a mistake? Stop expecting him to be perfect.

From a guy's perspective, being picked on over one thing when you feel you are doing a lot to make the relationship work feels like a kick in the guts. You feel underappreciated and you question why you are making such an effort in other areas just to be singled out over one thing. You can't help fearing what life might be like going forward with a person who seems to overreact over one setback while ignoring all that's good about you. It doesn't seem like a recipe for a happy life.

This is not to say you should let the guy get away with being a lazy slob who is expected to do nothing. If you are constantly nagging him or he fails to take initiative over the simplest of things, then you have an issue on your hands. In this situation you need to question whether you can see yourself having to put in all the effort to keep the relationship alive.

However, if you are with a generally good guy who is supportive towards you and shows he can take responsibility, sometimes the wisest course of action is to let things slide once in a while. Forgiveness is a virtue and an endearing quality that will be noticed by your other half: no doubt you can expect such generosity of spirit in return.

Another thing to remember is that at some stage in his life, his mother probably pointed at his faults. When he was entering his teenage years there was no doubt conflict over his behavior, habits and the things he did or did not do around the house. While that tension is a natural part of life for most families with children, you certainly don't want to be compared in his mind with an overbearing mother. That association will have him running for the hills!

So it's time to be the bigger person and cut the guy some slack.

CONCLUSION

So there you have it. The 40 things that men wish you knew.

I know that some of these ideas may sound controversial to you — or even downright offensive in some cases. But I also hope that, as you read through the book, you gained a new perspective on how the male mind operates. Perhaps this new knowledge gave you some insight into the obstacles you've experienced previously in relationships, and why your partner may have acted the way he did at the time.

As I said at the beginning of this book, my goal was not to give you a fluffy, pleasant or easy reading experience. That would have been a disservice to you, and a waste of the money you spent.

My goal was to drop some cold, hard truth bombs so that you are now armed with the knowledge to make different decisions going forward. My goal was also to give you an accurate perspective on how men think in relationships. This, of course, does not mean that you have to mold yourself to their every whim or desire. There's nothing to be gained from losing your true identity in a relationship.

However, I believe you are now equipped with a greater understanding of gender dynamics when it comes to successfully navigating the worlds of dating, courtship and maintaining a strong and stable relationship long into the future.

It's understandable if you resist some of these ideas, or just plain disagree with them. We all bring our unique upbringing, life experiences and beliefs to the table. What may not resonate with you at present may become more apparent as you gain more life experience.

Courtship and relationships can be a minefield of miscommunication, mismatched expectations and misunderstandings. Your partner's perspective could be vastly different to your own on any given issue. This book is designed to help bridge these gaps with down-to-earth, actionable advice.

I hope it has proved useful, and I sincerely wish you every success in your relationships going forward.

Jarred Jameson

CPSIA information can be obtained
at www.ICGtesting.com
Printed in the USA
LVHW080354110522
718463LV00027B/739